TRAVELS IN OUDAMOVIA

Travels
in
Oudamovia

John Austin Baker

Foreword by the Archbishop of Canterbury

THE FAITH PRESS
Leighton Buzzard, Beds, LU7 7NQ
MOREHOUSE-BARLOW CO. INC., NEW YORK, U.S.A.

FIRST PUBLISHED IN 1976

© *John Austin Baker, 1976*

PRINTED IN GREAT BRITAIN
in 10pt. Times type
BY THE FAITH PRESS LTD.
LEIGHTON BUZZARD LU7 7NQ
SBN 7164 0435 4

TO MY WIFE

FOREWORD

THIS book is the sharing of a vision, and I for one am immensely grateful to be in on the sharing.

Those of us who know Canon Baker's *The Foolishness of God* will approach this little Lent Book with high hopes, and we shall not be disappointed. It is not so stiff a book as the other, but who is to say that it is not as profound in its insights and in the questions which it asks? Under a deceptively simple guise, it touches on some of the main themes with which Christians are concerned—Incarnation, eschatology, ethics, education, man and nature, Eucharist among them.

I hope this book will be read slowly and thoughtfully by many this Lent. It would make an admirable basis for work in study groups.

✠ DONALD CANTUAR:

PREFACE

OF making of Utopias there is no end. An account of an imaginary society has for centuries been a useful way of re-asking fundamental questions, of trying to open up new options. It can also, if well done, satisfy deeper, emotional longings in both writer and reader.

This particular Utopia began twelve or more years ago in some sermons preached in the chapel of Corpus Christi College, Oxford. But the Oudamovia* of those days was outwardly, though not inwardly, a very different place—a spacious, high technology society, where the citizens walked everywhere on multi-lane moving roadways activated by linear accelerators. If that country has passed away, it was not because Christianity and technology proved irreconcilable; on the contrary, technology is a splendid way of realising one's theological fancies! The reasons were practical. I did not care to join the Space-travellers, and there was now nowhere to hide so large and well-stocked a country on this planet. So Oudamovia had to be small and remote and inevitably poor. Nor does the compass of a Lent Book leave much room for picturesque but dispensable detail. The result has been to force attention back to human problems which are with us always, and some of which become more urgent as our world becomes smaller, more denuded of resources, and nearer to disaster.

Lacking the skills of the novelist, I cannot hope to have written an exciting story, but at most to prompt the odd unfamiliar line of thought. I am deeply grateful for the privilege of having been asked to supply the Archbishop of Canterbury's Lent Book, and for his generosity in allowing me to bring people real and dear to me, if to no one else, into existence at last on the printed page.

JOHN AUSTIN BAKER

Westminster Abbey.
Lent 1976.

* From the Greek *oudamou,* meaning "nowhere".

One

WHERE is Eden? Behind us, always, the irrevocably lost: childhood summers, unnamed songs, first love. But Eden, whatever it may be for each one of us, must also lie ahead. It must somehow make its way into heaven, for if it does not, then even heaven will not be home.

This is the story of an Eden which came late. My being there at all was an inconceivable chance—or providence—and there can be no going back. But as sure as there is a heaven, and a merciful God to bring us there, we shall all of us find something of Oudamovia among the joys at that journey's end; and that is why I am trying my hand at this fragmentary and inadequate account. There are some joys for which it is as well to be prepared.

My name—does not matter. When all this happened, I was an Anglican clergyman not long retired from my last parish, a large residential village some thirty miles south of London. I had been very content there. The church was charming, basically fifteenth century, and in good repair. The congregation, mostly middle-class people, intelligent and interested, had been loyal and not too depressingly small. But the shadows were lengthening across the green of my days (I am a widower, and my marriage had been one of the lucky ones) and I was learning to go softly and not repine at all the things that now would never be done. Our only child, a daughter, was married and living in Africa. It was almost time anyway to bow out gracefully, and the decision was speeded by a sudden and completely unexpected windfall. One of my oldest friends, a man I had not seen for some years, for his health was poor and he lived much abroad, but with whom I still corresponded regularly, died; and in his will it was found that he had left me his week-end cottage "because", as he put it, "the clergy never have anywhere to live when they retire, and this is to encourage him to retire while he can still enjoy it, for his own good and everyone else's".

So I came to Dorset, to a tiny home of my own, tucked against the side of a hill just outside a small village, and looking south-west to the sun. A mile's walk down the rough road brought one to a quiet bay, where the water always seemed to be incredibly still, and took a strange sheen from the great slabs of grey slate running out from the foot of the cliffs. It was a walk I often made, especially in autumn and early spring when the visitors, never very many, were not about.

It was here, on an afternoon in late February, that the story really begins. I had stayed longer than usual, enjoying the silvery warmth one sometimes gets at that time of year in a suntrap between two rocks, and was more than ready for my tea. As I stood up and stretched myself and took a last look round I caught sight of a long, slim brown shape moving swiftly across the water not, as I thought, very far out. It puzzled me, being unlike any craft I could think of. Perhaps it was some secret naval or military vessel. Curiosity kept me standing there watching for some considerable time, and I realised that she was much larger and when first sighted had been a lot farther offshore than I had supposed. She was now close in, and revealed as a big catamaran with a low bridge-like structure forward on each hull, in which men were visible. The uncanny thing was that there was no noise of engines, only the sound of the low swell breaking against her. Suddenly it became apparent that she was slipping between the heads of the bay and running in toward the beach. Neither on the cliff-top nor on the shingle nor on the path was there a soul to be seen, and a shiver of fright ran over me. I felt exactly as I had done years ago in America, when a large bear came from nowhere, intent on its own affairs, and shambled by within fifty yards: freeze and hope not to be noticed.

The catamaran had now stopped, and was lying parallel to the shore, more or less in the centre of the bay. A deck hatch opened, and two men climbed out, bringing with them a canoe which they launched and began to paddle beachwards. I stared hypnotised. The sun was by now almost down, and the floor of the cove was in black shadow. Only high above our heads the fields were still bright, the sky a hazy blue. I had the absurd thought that all existence had been temporarily suspended, that all this was taking place in a momentary check in Time, and that only when whatever was in the doing had been done would the clock of the universe start oscillating again. I continued to stand immobile as the men beached their boat and set off round the curve of the shore toward me. It was obvious that they had spotted me, and that I was their objective. Totally passive, I waited for whatever was to happen. The men were ten feet away. They halted, and the taller of the two spoke. "Are you a Christian?"

On any expectations it was an odd question, and for a moment, completely baffled, I said nothing. From their accent the men were obviously foreigners; but they did speak English, and yet had no idea that a clerical collar was the dress of a Christian minister. (I am an old-fashioned clergyman, and have always resisted the fashion of so many of my colleagues of dressing as much like the laity as possible, having a suspicion that most people, unless they see clergy about, will assume that the Church is virtually extinct.) What, anyway, could they possibly want that would make this the natural way to open their enquiry? In the end it was, I suppose, a sort of automatic professionalism that made me stop acting like the village idiot—after all, whatever their reasons, they were on my own ground. They had not asked me for medical aid or diesel oil. After a discourteously lengthy pause I heard myself say, "Yes, I am. What can I do for you?"

The man who had first spoken now turned round, and waved to his friends in the ship, which at once began to turn and head out to sea. His companion stepped forward, put his arms on my shoulders, and kissed me.

"God be praised! Do you live near?"

"About a mile."

"May we speak with you?"

"Certainly. Come with me."

I led the way to the path and up on to the road, saying nothing more. Endless questions clamoured in my mind, but I felt awkward, and determined to wait until we were comfortably indoors and settled down. Also I was jumpy with embarrassment lest we meet any of my neighbours, and I might have to explain my new acquaintance, with their full, long-sleeved tunics, belted at the waist, white knee-length breeches, and sandals. The tunics were a vivid scarlet which stood out in the deepening dusk like life-saving jackets. But we met no one. Once safely inside the cottage, I stirred up the fire, sat them down with glasses of sherry, and announced my intention of preparing a meal. "Then we can talk," I said.

And talk we did, far into the night, and I learned the strangest tale that perhaps any man or woman alive has ever heard. I am not sure to this day why I believed it, or why, as the hours wore on, the whole incredible concatenation of circumstance came to seem entirely natural and even intended. This was the story that bit by bit, with many interruptions and incomprehensions on my part, eventually emerged.

They came, they said, from a country called Oudamovia, which had been cut off from all contact with the rest of mankind for seventeen hundred years, and only recently had they discovered how to break out of their isolation. The strange craft I had seen and its crew constituted their first foray back into the family of mankind; and it was not by chance that they had found their way at last, after a voyage of many thousands of miles, to the coast of England. This had been their goal from the start, since the English I heard them speaking was the only contemporary language, apart from their own, of which they had any knowledge (if indeed their brand of English could be called contemporary, since their vocabulary lacked all kinds of common words in use among us today). The explanation of this turned out to be that

14

several generations back a boat had been washed up on their shores in which, among other things, they had found a box containing a number of English books, and some ship's charts. How, you may wonder, had they managed to decipher them? The answer to that question brings us to the most startling part of the whole business: one of those books had been a Bible, *and the Oudamovians were Christians.*

Their almost incredible claim was that the original settlers of their island had been the descendants of Christian refugees from the Roman Empire of the mid-third century, at the time of the Decian persecution. Successive migrations had brought the last, tiny remnant of this heroic band to their present fastness in the far southern hemisphere, and there they had first survived, then prospered. For a long time they were puzzled that no other ships ever came in sight of their land; but after every attempt of their own to explore beyond the horizon came to disaster, their boats being lost without trace, they concluded that God meant them to be prisoners, and gave their whole mind to making the life of their community as self-sufficient as they possibly could.

In this way they had finally achieved a condition of great peace and contentment. But of recent years certain ominous signs had convinced them that their island was in imminent danger of being overwhelmed by natural catastrophe. At once a great debate began: was there any chance of escape? of finding a new home where they could start again? But in the end, after the whole nation had given itself to prayer, they came to a conclusion so remarkable, and so foreign to anything of which one could conceive our own society to be capable, that it was when I heard of it that all my doubts were dissolved and I became utterly convinced of the truth of everything they were telling me. The whole people of Oudamovia, young and old alike, had agreed that what God had given them in this world was so perfect that they had no right to try and secure its continuance beyond whatever term he might set to it. "Only in heaven", said Taddi (he was the smaller man of the two, the one who had kissed me), "could we hope to see more of himself than God has already

15

shown us, so why, if he calls us, should we run from him?"

Only one thing had grieved them. Before the end came they longed to see another Christian face, and to share with their brethren some of the joy they had known so abundantly. It was decided, therefore, to make one more attempt to find a way out through the terrible circle girdling their island, and to send messengers to the only other Christians of whom they had recent certain knowledge, the English. But they also determined, if successful, to act with circumspection, in case the world at large were still as hostile to the faith as the one they had left. They had no desire for their existence to become known to pagan powers, of which indeed the government of England itself might be one, who would then try to force a way through those natural hazards which had till now guarded Oudamovia's secret but which, if they themselves managed to get out, could obviously no longer be relied upon to do so.

In the end, after much sacrifice and trouble, they had solved the problems, and the arrival of their strange craft in our Dorset cove, unseen (thanks to some quirk of perverted divine humour) by any eyes except my own, was the climax of the adventure. But it had all taken so long to prepare that time was running out. The captain of the ship was even afraid that if they did not return immediately they might be too late. At this point a tidal wave of panic rose and swamped me. I could see so clearly the question that was coming, and I could not think of any worthy reason for refusing. "Will you come with us?" (it was Taddi speaking again). I sat silent. Then I temporised. "But if what you say is true, there would not be time for me to get back, and your message would be lost just as surely as if you had never come. Would it not be better to tell me as much as you can about Oudamovia, and let me write it all down, and I will promise to pass it on to as many other Christians as possible?" "It is not something that can be told", he replied, "you must have seen it with your own eyes, breathed it, tasted it, touched it, heard it." "O taste and see how gracious the Lord is!" I said half to myself. I looked round

16

the room. My home, which I had known so short a time, seemed to beg me not to leave it. But—"if he calls us, should we run from him?" Without any trace of consoling exaltation but with a heart like lead I heard myself answer, "Very well, I will come. But now I think we all need some sleep."

The ship was to return at the same time the following day. I made my visitors keep to their bedroom, and then I set about covering my absence. I cancelled the milk and the papers, told the woman who came in from the village that I had been invited away for a holiday abroad, and had the post redirected to my bank. There was the car to be jacked up, the electricity and water to turn off, the refrigerator to empty—the usual things. And also the unusual ones, mostly letters, including one to my solicitor enclosing a sealed message to be opened if he had not heard from me by the end of the year. The hardest to write was the letter to my daughter. Then to pack, just one bag.

The fine spell had broken, and the evening was grey and raw with a thin, sleety rain driving as we walked down the garden path and shut the little iron gate behind us. The lights were on up in the village, and I could hear Mrs. James calling her children in for their tea. I felt a longing to say good-bye to someone, anyone, but no one came past, which was all to the good. When we reached the cove the catamaran was already there. My companions carried the canoe down from the place behind the rocks where they had hidden it, and in a few minutes we were aboard. I said to myself, "All shall be well, and all manner of thing shall be well," but as the cliffs dropped slowly below the horizon it was not an easy thing to believe.

Two

OF our journey I can say little intelligently, and that little is by now irrelevant anyway. The voyage was a desperate and terrifying business, from which in the last stages I felt sure none of us would emerge alive. What was it that had imprisoned (or protected) Oudamovia for so long? As a layman it is impossible for me to say. The area around it is certainly alive with submarine volcanic disturbance and violent electric phenomena. Whether this produces some kind of masking effect, in addition to destroying any ships or planes that venture too close?—it hardly seems possible, especially in an age of satellite mapping, that even a relatively small piece of land, and one far from the usual sea and air routes, could wholly escape notice, yet the fact remains that it had. Anyhow, one thing I can vouch for, and that is that there is nothing mysterious at all in the failure of travellers through the centuries to reach the island. Our own vessel, which was a masterpiece of design and construction, and had been dedicated to Paul the Apostle in commemoration of the way in which his presence saved the Alexandrian ship taking him and his friends to Italy from foundering in the Adriatic, seemed doomed more than once. But in the end, exhausted and overjoyed, we made it.

It was one o'clock on Easter night when I caught my first sight of Oudamovia. We were gliding gently across a broad lagoon toward the capital, Lohir. From east to west the whole place was ablaze with the most enormous firework display I have ever seen.

First impressions are blurred by fatigue. Sounds, shapes, colours have all run into one another in my memory, and indeed made little sense at the time. We went straight from the ship on to a wide street rising gently from the quayside. Like the whole city it was filled with crowds of people, dressed in rich and radiant colours. Some were dancing in sets or singing while their friends accompanied them on wind or stringed instruments. Some were just strolling arm in arm, laughing and watching the fireworks. Others sat out at tables, eating and drinking, for the night air was quite unusually warm. Weary as I was, I remember thinking it strange that a people on the very lip of catastrophe should display not a hectic gaiety—that has been common enough in human history—but such a natural and unclouded happiness. The atmosphere was exactly that of a country village *en fête*.

As we reached the top of the slope from the harbour and joined a kind of boulevard, two huge balloons floated into view, carrying an inscription in large letters painted on their sides. Looking everywhere but where I was going, and still shaky from my sea-legs, I would have fallen had not my friends lifted me bodily. Clutching the arm of my nearest guide, I asked him why all the festivities? He looked at me in amazement. "Surely you know!" he said, "it's Easter Day!" "The Lord is risen", he added, pointing to the balloon-borne motto overhead.

After about ten minutes we turned into a fine garden, filled with the tingling night scents of shrubs and flowers. Passing up a flight of steps, we entered a large house, and were ushered into a long, plain room. From the far end a man who had been standing gazing out at the garden came forward to greet us. He was of medium height, slim, and with the dark hair and olive skin of all the Oudamovians, and he too had their normal serene and happy expression. At the same time this man's face expressed to an outstanding degree another quality, one which I had already learned to recognise in the companions of my journey, and which I can describe only as a directness and decisiveness that seemed to spring from some deep inner certainty. If you are lucky enough, as I have been, to have met from time to time any of that small number of men and women who are both well integrated and exceptionally holy, you will recognise what it is I am trying to identify. It shows itself most of all, perhaps, in their conversation. It is not that such people have no small talk; on the contrary they often take a more real interest and pleasure than others in the little things of ordinary life. But what they say, on these or any other topics, is disconcertingly free of the conventional insincerities and the clichés of mental laziness that pad out so much of the talk of most of us. They have a different scale of priorities which brings to their minds as the first and natural comment some truth about which you or I would perhaps be too shy (or care too little?) to speak. As he came toward me this was, I felt sure, just such a man.

It may be as well to interject here a word about Ouda-movian dress. For men the normal costume was the long belted tunic and a kilt; the knee-breeches of the sailors I had first met were characteristic only of certain occupations. At work, they have either a short sleeveless top, rather like a straight-bottomed waistcoat, tied with a single lace, or during the warmest months nothing at all. The women wear dresses to below the knee, looped up under the breasts. In the cold season, which was now almost due, both sexes use leggings, boots instead of sandals, and fleece-lined leather coats. But the most important feature of their clothing is the colour. Oudamovians love colour, and have developed a wonderful range of vegetable dyes both rich and delicate in shade. These colours, which had so struck me when I first landed, play a vital part in their social organisation. The whole population is divided into twelve clans, and each clan has its own basic colour. Your tunic, if you are a man, or your dress, if a woman, will be made of material dyed to your clan colour, and you will wear that all your life. (One very practical value of this rule relates to their marriage laws: no doubt to prevent too much inbreeding in a small population, no one may marry someone of the same clan; so, if you are wearing gold, you learn early to let your fancy roam among the other eleven colours!) But everyone is free to decorate their clothing with any colour or pattern they like, so long as the ground remains the same. Since no one is allowed to possess more than one change of clothing, great ingenuity and art is shown in making one's dress individual and beautiful; and by the use of appliqué designs, all worked at home, it is possible to change the decoration from time to time. The young take more advantage of this than their elders. The men in particular, though their tunics are often resplendent, tend, once they have found a design, usually symbolic, which satisfies them, to stick to it for the rest of their lives. Another Oudamovian custom is that there are no special robes to go with public office or position. This is rooted in deep convictions about the very nature of government and leadership; but in practice it is hard to imagine what ceremonial dress could possibly make any impact amid such a torrent of sensuous pattern and colour as any Oudamovian gathering displays.

The personage who now came up with hand outstretched, and clasped my forearm in a greeting not unlike that of ancient Rome, was therefore dressed in principle like any other citizen. His tunic, which showed him to be a member of the White clan, was embroidered up each side with winged animals in a deep coral red. Introductions were made. I knew already, from briefing on the ship, that this must be the Laiarch of Oudamovia, their head of state, an elective office held for only one year at a time and only once in a lifetime. In stilted English, no doubt learned for the occasion, but patently sincere, he gave me welcome:

"My friend, this is an unspeakable joy for us to meet after so long a man from another land who also walks in the peace of Christ. May you and your people always abide in him!"

"You know", he went on, "what great danger we are in. Perhaps it was wrong of us to bring you here. But you must forgive us. We have longed to break bread with a brother from beyond the sea, so that when we have gone hence there will be those who will pray for us and remember. I believe that we were right, that it was God's will, and that he who has brought you this far will return you safe to your own land. Meanwhile, on behalf of us all, I thank you for your courage and charity in coming so far and through such perils."

"There was not much courage about it", I replied. "My

own course is almost run, and I have had a good life. It will be a great blessing if I can return and tell of all I have seen here, but if not it will not greatly matter. We shall all meet in the end, and my people will one day know yours." At this point I suddenly swayed, and had to hold on to a table near the wall to save myself from falling. He sprang forward and supported me. As from a great distance I could hear him speaking, then the singing in my head swelled up and I remember no more till I awoke in bed in a cool, quiet room to see sunlight streaming though a deep embrasure at the far end and to hear the song of a bird. I had slept for more than twelve hours.

Three

MY hosts insisted on keeping me in bed until the next morning; but then, after breakfast in the Laiarch's garden, we settled down to plan the best way to make use of what might prove a rather limited stay. It was in the course of this conversation that I at last stumbled on the explanation of something that had puzzled me a great deal during the talks I had had with my companions on the voyage about Oudamovian life. This is a matter of such fundamental importance for understanding the rest of my story that I had better deal with it right at the start, compressing and putting in logical order points that in fact became clear to me only as the result of talks and experiences throughout my time in Oudamovia.

The difficulty of which I was conscious had arisen virtually every time I used the word "church". It was not that they did not know it; after all, it comes often enough in the New Testament. But whenever it came up, we seemed immediately to get at cross-purposes. This morning a perfectly innocent and, I think you will agree, natural remark of mine brought the whole problem out into the open. I simply said: "Perhaps the best way to start would be to visit one or two churches".

What emerged was not just a difference of usage or practice between us and them but of the whole perspective in which Christianity is understood. It was their total vision which was different from our own. And the significant thing, to my mind, was that it was different not because they had made any radical or revolutionary changes in the content of the Gospel; they had not. Here indeed was a people whose basic faith was, by the standards of our day, extremely orthodox and traditional. Despite their having been cut off from the rest of Christendom well before the creeds were

23

formulated—and they had never developed anything of the sort for themselves—they held in essence a trinitarian, incarnational faith. I think probably, recalling what I can of the lectures in my student days, that some of their ways of putting their beliefs were formally heretical; but their intention was clear enough. Possessing the same scriptures as ourselves, and starting no doubt from the ordinary teaching of the Christian community from which they had set out all those centuries ago, they still had a very "old-fashioned" Gospel; and they had not had the benefit of successive critiques of that Gospel, from Arius onwards, to help them change their minds. But they had read the meaning of this belief in a very distinctive way, and this had given them quite a new outlook on the world.

The core of their faith is a quite literal belief in what historically has been the central and peculiar tenet of the Christian religion: that in Jesus of Nazareth the eternal God knew our human existence as we ourselves know it. He lived a true human life and died a true human death. Since Jesus on earth prayed to his Father in heaven, they hold that though God is One, yet in himself he is also more than One. As for the Holy Spirit, they say: "No one has ever seen the Father. The Lord Jesus returned to the Father when his work on earth was done, and no one living has ever seen him. Yet both the Father and the Lord Jesus are our dear friends, with whom we talk day by day. This is the work of the Spirit, God with us, who, as the Apostle John records, we were told we should receive, and who would fulfil the prophecy of the Lord that the Father and the Son should come and make their home in our hearts."

The worries that beset so many other Christians to this day as to how such things can be, seem to have passed them by. They appear to lack interest in speculation or metaphysics; and when I tried to explain some of the controversies within our own tradition, their reaction may be fairly summed up in the words of one older Oudamovian, a grandmother in a village where I stayed: "There are things which I can do which to my youngest grandchild seem impossible. There

24

are many things in the world which seem to me impossible, but they happen. How can a man foretell the future? How can a woman be in one place and yet see something happening in another place? But we all know these things are true. If we were beyond the world, perhaps we would see the whole, and understand why they are quite easy. Perhaps from where God is one could see that it is even easy for him to be one of us. I do not know. But I do know that a thing is not impossible just because it seems to me impossible."

It would be quite wrong, however, to conclude from this that the Oudamovians are totally credulous, and will believe anything just because, let us say, it is written in scripture. It is rather that the tests they apply are different from those we use. What they ask about something is whether it is right, whether it is morally fitting. And this is their ultimate reason for believing in the Incarnation: it seems to them morally necessary if they are to believe in God at all. The argument, as they explained it to me, goes something like this.

"To believe in God is to believe in a good God; for if that which sits in God's throne is not good, then there is no 'God', because there is nothing eternal which is worthy of our worship. But the world is much in bondage to pain and evil, and sorrow as well as joy is built into the nature of things. How then does God show himself good in respect of the sufferings of his creatures?

"He does not show himself good by enabling us to understand, so that we may endure our sufferings willingly and with confidence that they are the necessary means to a good end. The efforts of the wise and the inspiration of prophets alike have failed to find the explanation. We can guess at partial reasons but we never divine the meaning of it all. This does not show that there is no meaning. Just as some things seem to us impossible because we cannot stand beyond the whole and see all its possibilities, so some things seem to us meaningless because we cannot stand outside the whole and see the pattern of its meaning. But this in itself is part of the suffering God imposes on us. We are creatures who cannot

25

help hunting for understanding any more than a wild animal can help hunting for its prey. But in this matter God has doomed our nature to frustration; and if he does so for our good, then by that very fact he prevents us from knowing that this is so. So it is not here that God shows himself good in respect of suffering.

"He cannot show himself good by grieving over our sorrows from his throne in heaven. Even if he could prove to us that his heart was grieved (and from heaven he cannot), it would not be enough. He would be like an Emperor who stays in his palace, and sends his armies to certain death, they know not why. Perhaps in the night he weeps for them and cries out, and sleep refuses to come to him. Perhaps in his thoughts he lives through their wounds and cold and hunger. But if someone visits the army and tells them how unhappy he is, what will they say? That he is a good man, and they are glad to die for a man like that? Of course not! They will spit, and say, 'Too bad! we're really sorry for him, the poor bastard! If he's so upset, let him come out here and try the real thing!'

"There is only one way in which, with the world as it is, God can show himself good in respect of man's suffering; and that is by not asking of us anything that he is not prepared to endure himself. He must share the dirt and the sweat, the bafflement and the loneliness, the pain, the weakness, yes, and the death too. That would be a God one could respect, a God who put aside all his magic weapons, and did it all as one of us. A God who, when we cry out in our misery (as we all do), 'Why should this happen to me?' can answer truthfully, 'It happened to me too, not because I couldn't help it happening, but because I chose that it should, because it was right'. Then and then alone will our doubts be stilled, not because we understand, but because we can trust."

That, then, was why the Oudamovians believed in the Incarnation, even though they had no more idea than anyone else how the thing was done: because it makes supreme moral sense. They did not imagine that this "argument" proved either God's existence or that he became man. They knew as well as you or I do that God cannot be "proved", because anything that could be proved would not be God. But their sense of the moral fitness of things told them that a God who became Man was the only God in whom they could believe with rational and moral integrity; and since they still thought God the best ultimate explanation of existence, the Christian account of God seemed to them obviously the true one. Their historical traditions about the ancient world from which they came meant that they were not at all surprised by what I could tell them of other religions in the world today. But what utterly puzzled and astounded them was to learn that some Christians wanted to give up belief in God's becoming man. "Don't worry too much, though", they said to me, "reason will prevail in the end".

Now this was in substance, as I say, a very conventional and old-fashioned faith, even if their reasons for holding it were somewhat different from the usual ones. But the interesting thing was that the conclusions they drew from it, the way it made them look at life, were not the conventional ones of Christendom at large. Yet they started off safely enough: because the Son of God has become man, all men and women are brothers and sisters of the Son of God. Is this not after all simply a message the New Testament repeats over and over again? Or is it?

You see, when they said that "all men and women *are* brothers and sisters of the Son of God", they meant it. They did not mean that all men and women now have the opportunity to become brothers and sisters of the Son of God by taking the appropriate steps, professing the Christian faith and joining the Christian community. This relationship to the eternal Son is a fact about all human beings—atheists, pagans, Jews, Buddhists, Muslims, Hindus, voodooists, the lot—whether they realise it or not. It is something that has been done for them unilaterally by the Son's becoming man, long before they were born.

"In this", the Oudamovians ask, "is not the family of God just like any human family?" Each one of us is born into an already existing human family without our consent. Our relations are given to us; we do not choose them. That is why they are so good for us—they teach us the necessity of Christ's law, "Love your enemies", a law without which human society cannot hope to survive! What we do with our family, however, is up to us. We may use it as God's gift, a chance to learn to love, to work together, to forgive, to understand, all to the limit, and so grow up into something like Christ's own stature. Or we may choose to gird against our fate, to hate or despise our kinsfolk and be estranged from them. That is our decision. What is not our decision is to find our way into the family. We start there.

So it is with mankind. All are in God's family, because his Son is one of us. We could never have got ourselves into such a good family, nor can we now cancel the fact that we do belong to it. All we can do is disown it, be alienated from it, reject its values, go off on our own, and pretend we do not belong. "What, after all", they asked me, "did you think the story of the Prodigal Son was about?"

Naturally enough, therefore, they had no need for our conception of the Church. In their eyes everyone was already and automatically in the divine community, and the whole human race was the Body of Christ. To them it made no sense at all to have some group smaller than the race claiming that people have to belong to that in order to become brothers and sisters of the Son of God. Such a claim seemed to them ridiculous and illogical; and the more I discussed it with them, questioning them about the New Testament and its teaching that all men have to make an act of faith in Jesus as Lord and be baptized in order to be saved, the more certain they became that they were right and our interpretation was wrong. "No wonder you get into such muddles about Paul and his teaching of faith not works", they said to me. "Your interpretation is bound to turn everything into works, because you say that there is still something we have to do, some contribution we have to make, in order to achieve the state of salvation and become children of God. For you, faith is the one work needful. But people do not

28

have to do anything. It is all grace. It is not even that there is a door which Christ has unbolted, and we, standing outside it, have to stretch out our hand, lift the latch, and walk through. We are already inside. When our Saviour became man and undid the sin of Adam, he did not command the cherubim with the flaming sword to return to heaven so that we could re-enter Eden. He picked up the walls of Eden and carried them to the farthest edge of Ocean, and there set them up so that they now girdle the whole world. All we are asked to do is to open our eyes and recognise where we are. Once we have done that, then we shall look down at ourselves and our filthy bodies and our tattered clothes, and we shall say, 'I am not fit to be here, in Paradise'; and we shall ask for baptism to wash us clean, and for the white robe of chrism to clothe us in the righteousness of the Lord. But not in order that we may be saved—simply because this is fitting for those who have been saved."

It is not difficult, of course, to see how the Oudamovians grew into this frame of mind. For seventeen hundred years they lived in a world where Christianity was every man's native air. Never in all that period did a serious rival arise to challenge it. There were, it is true, those in Oudamovia who did not accept the faith. They were the rebels, the non-conformers, rejecting what everyone else took for granted. They were not persecuted or penalised. They were treated just like difficult members of a family, still kith and kin however they chose to behave. This must, I think, have been their most galling possible hardship, the calm assumption by almost everyone that they were really being rather silly, no doubt for reasons they could not help, and were beyond all question totally wrong. It is always infuriating when the virtues for which you think you ought to be hated are regarded by others as the faults despite which they insist on loving you.

As for the New Testament references to the Church, the *ekklesia*, the Oudamovians said this was a purely neutral and factual term, denoting in every case simply the physical number of professing Christians, either in one particular place or throughout the world, whether assembled for some purpose such as worship or just living their ordinary lives. Since my return I have gone into this with some care. I do not think they were wholly right, but it is only in Ephesians that they seem to me certainly wrong. Nor do I think St. Paul had really got quite as far in his argument as they appeared to infer from some of his exploratory ideas, though one can see how these ideas might be extended to arrive at their own position. But such technical objections of scholarship would not have bothered them much. For them the truth that mattered was always the truth they themselves saw now as a result of the light thrown on their own experience of life by the faith once delivered to the saints. And if their truth now did not always seem to tally with the truth as expressed by Christians past, they did not disown or condemn that past—on the contrary, they did their best to cherish the memory of it so that it might act as a check on their extravagances and a stimulus to their limitations— but neither did they work themselves into a frenzy of guilt nor change their minds.

Four

OBVIOUSLY then there was no such thing in Oudamovia as "church life" as distinct from "ordinary life". Once this point had been made clear, planning my programme became fairly easy. What mattered was to see as much as possible of Oudamovia in every aspect. We decided to start with a quick look at Lohir itself.

The buildings of the city were of modest, human scale, lying amidst groves of high, feathery trees. Everywhere there were flowering shrubs, ranging in colour from the exquisitely pale and delicate to the most arrogantly gorgeous. The whole effect was extraordinarily delightful, and as we left the grounds of the Laiarch's house and returned to the boulevard I could not help wondering whether the large numbers of people walking briskly hither and thither were all on some absolutely necessary errand. I felt that if I worked in Lohir I would have managed to have quite a number of urgently necessary appointments in other parts of the city almost every day.

We had not been walking for more than a few minutes, however, when a deep rumbling like distant thunder caused me to look skywards. I now became aware for the first time that to the west of the city rose a sheer mountain wall, punctuated left and half-right by the truncated cones of two typical volcanoes. In the Laiarch's garden these had been hidden from us. Now their presence, looming and pitiless, felled my spirits at a single blow. At last I sensed the brooding destiny with which my hosts had learned to live every minute of their lives, and the thought of their serenity and happiness brought a lump to my throat. Then the voice of one of my guides, whose name was Barnabas, broke in on my self-indulgence:

"That noise was not one of the mountains you can see.

Beyond that one on the left there is another which runs straight down into the sea. That one has been very angry for some days now, so I expect it was that we heard."

"How many volcanoes are there?"

"Eight, so far as we know. Five on the western side, and three on the east."

"How big is the island?"

"Where we are going there is a great map. It will be easiest to show you everything there."

A moment later we turned off the roadway, and crossing over a stone footbridge walked up a side street. At the end of this was an archway leading into a large square garden surrounded on three sides by a white building. Many people were constantly passing in and out of the various wings of this building, which proved to be the Assembly House. We entered the central block, and there in the hallway, covering half the floor, was a gaily painted relief model of Oudamovia.

The island is square in outline on the south, spreading out along the north shore, and appears to be formed by the convergence of two chains of volcanic peaks. One runs from the north-east tip to the middle of the south coast; this is the line of mountains of which I had just seen a part. The other, shorter chain is bow-shaped, curving in from the north-west and out again at the south-west corner of the island. The mountains thus divide the country into three areas. On the east side there are foothills covered with trees sloping down to a small coastal plain. This district is covered with small settlements, in one of which I was shortly to stay. Here most of the farming was done. The central area, between the mountain chains, was hourglass-shaped. The broader northern half rested on the shore of the lagoon, and was largely filled with Lohir and its outlying houses. The waist of the hourglass and part of the southern half was occupied by a deep lake; and the rest of the southern section was a low-lying volcanic plain. The whole of this central area, right down to the outskirts of Lohir itself, abounded in hot springs, deep volcanic fissures, and wells of boiling mud; and even the water of the lake itself was hot from the continual eruptions along its floor. The western area was a narrow ribbon of land along a great curving bay, where the fisherfolk of Oudamovia had their tiny villages. The capital was linked to the western and eastern areas by a single road in each case, running over a high pass in the mountain wall on that side. The extreme measurements of the island were twenty-nine miles from west to east by roughly twenty from north to south. Because of the shape, however, I estimated the total area as little more than two hundred and thirty square miles, or very much the same as the Isle of Man; and of this only about seventy-five square miles was habitable.

The resources of the island were naturally limited, and since the Oudamovians could not get away from it, and other people could not get through to it, there was no possibility of supplementing them from elsewhere. The most notable lack was of mineral deposits. In common with other volcanic areas of the earth's surface Oudamovia had no resources whatever of ore to supply them with metal. The first settlers had had the metal implements and weapons they brought with them, but once these were worn out they had to find other techniques. Over the centuries they had shown the most incredible ingenuity in achieving results with wood and stone, from delicate eating knives of spar with ironwood handles to fine-bore stone conduits, glazed on the inner surfaces, for transmitting the boiling water from the volcanic springs.

The to us well-nigh unimaginable handicaps under which they had always laboured had given the Oudamovians certain inviolable rules and deep-rooted habits of mind. The first was a total rejection of waste in any shape or form. When raw materials are so scarce, and when fashioning them to one's needs is a process requiring enormous time, skill and patience, everything has to be made to last, and once made has to be looked after with the utmost care. In homes I visited it was commonplace to find tools which had been in use for a hundred years; and once I was shown a mirror, made by fusing some mineral on a black stone disc and mounting the whole on a wooden back, which was still in excellent con-

33

dition and regular use after more than a thousand years. Moreover, the decision to make any article calling for materials in short supply could never be taken by an individual; each item had to be sanctioned by the council of elders in the settlement, or in the case of larger projects by the Assembly in Lohir. Such rigid discipline was utterly essential to their survival.

Another fundamental feature is their attitude to time. Before I went to Oudamovia I had never realised how quickly we in our modern high technology world expect everything to be done. In fact this is a deeply significant spiritual change. We take it for granted that when we begin something we shall, barring accidents and unless we are already old, see it completed. The self-denying humility and sheer faith needed to plan and put in hand, for example, a great Gothic cathedral are qualities with which we find it difficult to identify imaginatively because we never need to develop them. Buildings of far greater size, if not beauty, can be thrown up in two or three years; and that is our scale. We become seriously impatient if it is exceeded. We expect six-lane motorways, costing a million pounds a mile, to be laid from one end of the country to the other almost as easily as if it were a matter of painting them on a wall-map with a brush. How can we even start to understand the, yes, the heroism of mind which built the roads of the Empire, thousands of miles of hewn and fitted stone from Scotland to Syria?

This heroism the Oudamovians had to acquire to a supreme degree. They came from a world where civilisation had attained a high level of technical sophistication. They knew what life could be like; but they were robbed of almost every means of realising that ideal. There was none of that slave labour which made the ancient world possible; to devise and construct the equipment for a particular piece of work could now take as long as the work itself would have taken in their homeland. All these things called for a long perspective and a sustained subordination of the individual to the corporate vision. But what makes their achievement especially remarkable was that they maintained this

34

perseverance and self-discipline knowing that at any moment their whole society might be snuffed out like one of their own tallow candles. Somehow they had to find the faith to work to a long time-scale while being only too vividly conscious that there might be no time at all.

For many centuries they had been aware that the very existence of the island was precarious, poised as it was like the lid on a titanic infernal cauldron. Every Oudamovian child had to learn to come to terms with this as a fact of life. Now few things are more corrosive of a people's morale than this sort of uncertainty. Those who have worked, for example, in southern Bangladesh have testified to this effect of imminent and anticipated catastrophe. How had the Oudamovians managed to avoid a general apathy and paralysis of the will which would have been quite as fatal to the community in the long run as any natural disaster?

They themselves were in no doubt about the answer. It was because that part of a primitive Christian faith which we commonly find least usable was for them the most relevant of daily realities: the doctrine of the End. For them, their predicament was but one instance of a universal principle; and they were in no worse case than any other man, woman or child in the whole world. Because the terminus of history was a matter which God had reserved to his own power, it was simply a given circumstance of all human life that plans had to be made always in the consciousness that it might never be possible to carry them out. What was true of the whole created order held good in little for each individual and each community. But because beyond the End lay not annihilation but God, there was no reason to give way to inertia or despair. If it was a Judge who stood at the door, this meant that nothing good would ever be eternally lost. Work that was worthy would be taken in some way into the glory of the kingdom, and therefore even one talent must not be allowed to lie idle but applied to some creative use, however small. What mattered in life was not success or achievement but a right intention and right action in pursuit of that intention, so that whenever the hour did strike they would not need to be ashamed. In short, having to live from day to day had ingrained in them the conviction that the end did not justify the means, indeed that the means was if anything more important. And if that is what the "eschatological" element, rightly understood, does to religious faith and life, then I can only say that I wish we had more of it.

This convergence of the teaching of the Gospel with the hard facts of life had also imbued them with the firm belief that on any disputed point the faith, and not human wishful thinking, would turn out to be the realistic and reliable wisdom. As a result their religious vision of the world helped to shape many decisions which we would regard as purely secular, whether these were taken in family conclave or in the little councils of elders that ran their villages or in the supreme assembly of the nation. Oudamovians had no need of bishops to sit in a House of Lords or to write to *The Times* to put the Christian position on this or that issue. The positions they took were naturally Christian positions because they thought spontaneously as Christian people. They were quite shocked to learn that we had academic experts in ethics who did nothing but live in universities and read and write books. "How can you", they asked indignantly, "leave anything so important as right and wrong and the practical fulfilment of the will of God to people who have no practical responsibilities?"

One final characteristic of Oudamovian life is perhaps of particular interest. You might suppose that the need to cultivate such a degree of detachment with regard to the precariousness of human affairs, and the hard struggle required to achieve any but the simplest level of civilised life, would have left them rather dour and sombre in temperament. Yet it was obvious that they had in fact created a very charming and relaxed type of human society. They had an eye for beauty; they loved colour and music; and, as I was to see, they lost no opportunity for celebration. The sense of how frail was their hold on all good things, and that they could never hope here for a continuing city, seemed to have given them a keener appreciation of life and a determination

36

to make the very best of every day and hour that might remain. In the Oudamovian soul, "Eat, drink, and be merry, for tomorrow we die", rang not as pagan folly and cynicism but as the highest Christian commonsense.

The reason for this, however, was not any doubt about the fact of life after death nor any uncertainty as to its character. On the contrary,

> "the shout of them that triumph,
> the song of them that feast"

was in their minds the most assured of expectations. But they regarded this not as a compensation for inevitable misery here but as God's ideal to which all existence ought to try to conform as nearly as might be. They were in fact believers in pleasure—not at the cost of goodness, needless to say, but as the proper consummation of goodness. They were inclined to harp on such texts as, "At thy right hand there are pleasures for evermore", and, "I came that they might have life, and have it more abundantly"; and they seem never to have given a ready hearing to that peculiarly Christian form of doubletalk which takes "life" in such passages to mean a special spiritual life that thrives on mortification, or "pleasure" to be a special joy which consists in hurling oneself on suffering or being wholly absorbed in the intellectual contemplation of theological truths. Life, joy, pleasure, all imply in their view that state of total well-being in which full-blooded enjoyment, involving the mind and all the senses, is alone possible.

This vitality went back, no doubt, in part to their very origins. When they first migrated, Christianity was still having to struggle internally (as she has had to do, off and on, ever since) against tendencies to extreme asceticism. There were those, for example, who even tried to say that if you were a real Christian you would never marry. Others, over-reacting against the vicious elements in pagan culture, were violently hostile to education or any of the arts. It is clear that the earliest Oudamovians did not belong to any of these groups. Instead they were of those who echoed God's own verdict on the world, that it is very good; and where the world seemed no longer to deserve that verdict, they saw this as something which it was Man's duty to put right.

If I have dwelt at some length on this rather abstract characterisation of the Oudamovian outlook on life, it is because this seems the best way of helping you to catch something of the human quality of my experiences among them during the weeks that followed. All that I have said of them remained true right up to the final horrendous close; and if there are any of you who succumb easily, as I do, to fear and anxiety, perhaps this story may help you, as my adventure has helped me, to exorcise these demons. For I am quite sure now that if the Gospel does not live up to our expectations, it is because we expect from it the wrong things, and put obstacles in the way of its power.

Five

WE spent the rest of that day walking around Lohir. The Oudamovians were perforce great walkers, having no draught or riding animals, nor any mechanical methods of transportation. The crippled, aged or infirm were taken about in vehicles reminiscent of the old-fashioned Bath chair, one friend pulling in front by means of a harness over the shoulders, another pushing from behind. The rest walked with an easy untiring stride, swinging from the hips, the trunk upright and the weight well centred. On the voyage over I had abandoned my own brown Oxfords for their open sandals, and certainly felt the benefit of the change; but even so I was hard put to it to keep up with them as the afternoon wore on. It was therefore with something like dismay that I learned we were to set off early the next day for a farming settlement called Beresit in the west of the island. The thought of crossing that formidable mountain wall by the pass I had seen on the map in the Assembly House was worrying.

In the event there was nothing to worry about. I had forgotten how small the island was. Even with the zigzag ascent up the steep western side of the mountain chain the whole distance was no more than fourteen miles, and we took it easily, reaching our destination about an hour before sunset, after stopping on the way to eat and rest.

The settlement in which we now found ourselves stood in the forest which ran in a wide belt along the eastern flank of the mountains. There were only four homes, but between them they housed some eighty people.

All Oudamovian homes were built on the same pattern. There was a large compound, surrounded on three sides by a continuous range of low, single-storey buildings, fronted by verandahs. These were in fact a series of small individual dwellings, the whole system being occupied by members of one family group: a grandfather and grandmother, let us say, their children with their wives and husbands, and the grandchildren, some of them also with wives and husbands. There would also be one or two vacant units kept ready at all times for guests or travellers. The open space in the middle always had a garden with grass and shrubs and small ornamental trees. In Lohir there was often a pool, fed by a continuous stream of warm water brought down in conduits from the hot springs behind the city. Because the compound was three-sided, it could be extended if the need arose. In the city, where the site often did not allow of this, a second storey might be added to part of the buildings, with its own gallery looking over the garden, and reached by an outside stair. But this was only of necessity. Oudamovians never felt happy living off the ground.

Who might join any particular home was an open matter. More often than not a wife on marriage would go to her husband's family compound, but this was by no means invariable. If the husband had to work in a particular area, he would be received into his wife's family home, or a couple might move from one home to another for a few years if their help were needed, or if there were more spare rooms in another place. Sometimes it happened that a family group almost died out, leaving only two or three elderly people and perhaps an infant. In that case they were always taken into another home to which they were connected by marriage; and there the seniors would be accorded the status of grandparents, for the Oudamovians pay special respect to the old.

By such means as these they managed to avoid some of the personal tragedies which seem to beset our own society. No one in Oudamovia ever had to end his or her days in loneliness or shut away with others like himself waiting for death. The situation of the old was in fact as nearly ideal as possible. They had their privacy when they wanted it, but the company of their own flesh and blood when they wanted that. They had the pleasure of their grandchildren without being overtaxed by them; and the equal pleasure of reminiscing with their contemporaries when they had had enough

40

of the present day. If they had no children, they were provided with a vicarious family, and accorded as much respect as if they had. They were sure that when they became ill or frail they would be looked after without being a burden, because there were many hands to share the work.

For the young too the system had its great advantages. When they were small, there were always other children to play with, in adolescence friends and elders to receive confidences and to ease the tensions of the parent-child relationship. When they got married and had children of their own, they could have their times of relaxation, because there were always other responsible adults to share the task of keeping an eye on the various offspring. And usually there were older people to consult without having to go all the time to one's own parents.

But best of all, perhaps, especially for so gregarious and sociable a people, there was the corporate life of the home or settlement. The evening I arrived at Beresit everyone sat round after supper, the older folk on their verandahs, wrapped up against the encroaching chill of autumn. Some mothers were chatting and doing various jobs, one sewing with a needle made with almost unbelievable delicacy out of wood, another spinning wool. The family to which I had come was that of Barnabas, my guide in Lohir and a man to whom I already felt myself drawn as if to an old friend. He had introduced me to some of the men of his own age, and was interpreting for me as we talked. The youths and older girls were playing a game rather like deck quoits, only with a flat disc, while the small children romped at a kind of Tag.

There was a guest that night, a man from a homestead near the north shore of the island who was on his way to Lohir. He was famed as a singer, and after a time people wandered over from the other houses on the settlement and asked to hear him sing. He went to his room and came back with a small harp-shaped instrument with nine strings, the range of which he increased by stopping the strings with a wooden wedge held in his left hand. His voice was a light tenor, quiet and haunting, though the music itself was diffi-

41

cult for me at first, and of course I could not follow the words at all. The tonality and melodic line reminded me, if of anything, of some of the older synagogue chants. I asked Barnabas afterwards what the song had been about, but he only shook his head and said it was too hard to translate.

After the song, however, which was greeted with a long, deep-throated "Aah!" of appreciation by the audience, came the Tale-telling. I give it a capital letter to signify, what I only learned later, that this was an Oudamovian institution. For the children it served the purpose of a bedtime story, but the adults also stayed and listened to it with rapt attention, though they must all have heard it many times. The narrator was the head of the family, Barnabas's father, Thomas. (One thing about Oudamovia it is easy to convey without distortion is their names, since so many of them were in fact New Testament or early Christian names.) Barnabas and I sat at the back at his suggestion. I was afraid he would not hear, but he reassured me:

"My father has the gift of speaking. In the Assembly he has often lowered his voice to a whisper, yet five hundred people have heard every word. If we sit here at the back I can translate for you without disturbing the others."

So he did, giving me a quick summary every other sentence or so. And as the tale went on my heart stood still and my eyes swam with tears, for it was the story of Perpetua and her friends, martyred under Septimius Severus in North Africa almost eighteen centuries ago, a story which can still be read today. Here was living proof, across what must have seemed to anyone an almost unbridgeable gap of time and space and culture, that we belonged, these people and I, to one another. We traced ourselves to a common fount, shared a common tradition. But what moved me most was something else: that this story which for me was just that, a "tradition", something written in a book to be read with antiquarian interest and a generalised human sympathy, was for them much much more, the memory of those who had actually been their forefathers' friends. These heroic souls were people their own family had known, or known of at near hand, and almost the last they had known before they vanished into the void and cut themselves off for ever. The note in Thomas's voice was true nostalgia, the pain of longing for return to the homeland, and it had never died.

I was not sufficient of a patristic scholar to be sure at the time how close old Thomas's telling kept to the tale as we have it preserved in the *Passio Perpetuae,* and in any case I had to rely on Barnabas's whispered sub-titles. Since my return I have tried to check with the text, and so far as I can make out the tradition seems to have been kept remarkably intact. But this is not surprising, since the Oudamovians attached the very greatest importance to the cultivation of the memory.

I saw something of this the very next day. Soon after sun-up the men dispersed to their farming. The women, I supposed, would be busy cooking and looking after the house and garden; and the best thing for me seemed to be to go off for a walk to keep from under their feet, and to see what I could see. But while some of the women were doing the usual things that have to be done the world over, the others, I noticed, were rounding up the children in the garden for lessons. So I stayed and watched.

Oudamovian children were never sent to school in the sense of an institution separate from the home, set up specially for educational purposes and with a staff of professional teachers. As a people they believed that there were two kinds of knowledge: the knowledge everyone ought to have, and the special wisdom any given individual might require in order to do the particular job allotted to him in the community. It was the job of the family to pass on to its young people the first kind of knowledge. "After all", Barnabas said to me, "if you have it yourself surely you can tell it to someone else. If you can't tell it, then probably you haven't acquired it properly yourself. Besides", he added with a grin, "having to teach it to the children stops us forgetting it!"

This method was, of course, possible only because the circumstances of Oudamovian life had cut out most of the subjects that feature in our own school curricula. The history and geography of the rest of the world, for instance, were a complete blank to them, as were foreign languages, except for the few who had unravelled English for the reasons I have related. Literature, science, art, mathematics were confined to what their ancestors had known when they migrated plus whatever the Oudamovians themselves had created or discovered. What was taught was, therefore, in the nature of the case very different from our idea of a basic education. But that did not mean that there was not a great deal to learn.

Two great principles provide the key to understanding their whole approach to education. The first is that we should learn what we need to know; and the second, that to learn something is to make it indelibly a part of oneself.

The first of these principles may seem obvious but it is not. How much of the content of the schooling in our own society is there because the children need to know it, and how much because some ideal theory of the kind of individual we want to create suggests that it would be a good thing to know this or that or to have this or that skill? Certainly the best kind of knowledge is more than the mere acquisition of facts; it is the placing of facts in a framework of understanding. But human beings vary greatly in their intelligence and ability to absorb. If then we want to do our best for all children, we must start by teaching them to understand and assimilate what is essential, so that the less able spend their limited capacity on things that really matter.

The Oudamovian notion of what really mattered was, needless to say, not quite the same as ours. A European child brought up among them would undoubtedly be handicapped when he came back to live here. But not all the differences related to what we may call the technical requirements of the two cultures. Some were matters of value. Thus, the Oudamovians admired above all things the capacity to be articulate. Right from the start the children were exercised constantly not just in speaking the language correctly but in expressing their thoughts fluently, clearly and coherently. A

44

good speaker, man or woman, was much admired and wielded great influence, so that the young grew up to think of this skill as something to be desired and striven after. By contrast, writing was not an art form at all. It was merely a practical necessity, a means of recording complex data of a temporary nature or of sending messages which for one reason or another the messenger would be unable to remember. No one in Oudamovia ever tried to convey anything of a personal nature, condolences, let us say, or an apology, or a declaration of love, by means of a letter. "The written word", Thomas said to me once, "says either too much or too little. It has no voice or hands, no smile or frown of its own, but only what the reader sees in his own heart." "But surely", I replied, "it is not easy to show truthfully what one feels or thinks, even speaking face to face?" "No", he answered, "it is not easy. That is why it has to be learned. God has given us the means of making ourselves known to each other, but we have forgotten how to use them. Perhaps in Eden we knew without being taught, and in heaven we shall know even as we are known. But now we have to work at it."

"But one may not know oneself the truth of what is in one's own heart."

"You are right. We have to learn that too. Of all our duties in this life there is none harder than speaking the truth."

Of the other subjects taught to the young child perhaps the most familiar to us would have been mathematics. But this was confined to the simplest arithmetical operations, which were of course carried out with the old Roman numerals. I had often wondered how arithmetic was done on that system, and it was fascinating to watch. I felt sorry for the children in this, for though there was in fact a logical method to it, it was slow and difficult to grasp at first, and multiplication and division were extremely cumbersome, even with the aid of an abacus-like calculator. In practice little time was given to this subject, once the rudiments of number had been learned. More advanced skills were taught later in life to those whose particular jobs made them necessary.

A great deal of time, on the other hand, was devoted to teaching them the laws of their country. There was a kind of code of fundamental law which every citizen had to know by heart. When disputes arose, the elders of the community would then arbitrate by applying whichever laws were relevant in the case in question, and resolving the conflicts between them as best they could and in the light of earlier judgments. Quite a large crowd of people would attend a case; and since they all knew the fundamental laws word for word, the arguments were followed with keen interest. Before a verdict was given, a general invitation was issued to anyone present to speak if he or she had anything pertinent to add to what the principals had already said; and not infrequently someone would bring up a case bearing on the dispute or offence, which had not already been mentioned. It was a leisurely business, but it meant that justice was a living concern of every Oudamovian, and this interest was fostered from their earliest years.

As you would expect, the same kind of intensive training was given in their religion, but in this case the material was restricted to the very simplest elements of the faith. There was no Bible study, as we know it, simply because there were no copies of the Bible readily available. The children were told a selection of biblical stories, strung on a very simple thread: that God had made the world good, and placed man in it to act as his agent to care for it; that man, while still ignorant and inexperienced, had imagined that he knew what was best simply by the light of his own intelligence; that in consequence men had committed every kind of folly and wickedness imaginable; that by various means and individuals God had brought them on to see something of their true vocation and their own shortcomings; that when the time was ripe his Son had come and lived as a Man among men, and that as a result of his life, death and resurrection our hearts had been freed and our eyes opened, so that now we could live as we should in this world and enjoy eternal happiness in the next. The heart of all this was, understandably, the story of Jesus and the main elements of his teaching. I spotted some incidents from apocryphal gospels, but in the main it was straight Matthew, Mark, Luke and John, and with remarkably little psychological elaboration or in-filling of the story, and certainly no sentimentality. Traditional explanations of Jewish customs would be included, for example, not always correct ones either; but that was all. The Old Testament was laid under contribution, apart from the stories of the creation and fall, really only to show how stupid and wicked mankind had been, except for God's chosen agents and teachers. Of Paul and others there was virtually nothing apart from stories from the Acts of the Apostles, supplemented again by apocryphal material, to show a pattern of Christian discipleship. Various apocalyptic elements rounded off the whole, this being, as I have said, a part of the faith that spoke particularly to the Oudamovian situation.

The children were expected to memorise these stories, and be able to tell them back; but no attempt was made to get them to think about them or draw any conclusions of their own. All that side of things was left to be done in the context of their worship, which I shall try to describe later. All that was attempted in their schooling proper was to imprint upon them the bare bones of the salvation story to carry with them for the rest of their lives.

Everything else in the children's instruction was purely practical. They were taught how to use various tools, and how to survive in the open; to observe the stars and the weather signs; to care for animals; what to do when people were sick; and so on. Only one idea might be thought not strictly utilitarian, though from their point of view it was, and that was the history and poetry of Oudamovia. The struggles and achievements of the pioneers in particular were told in traditional form—I was reminded strongly more than once of schooling in the United States of America—though not absurdly idealised. Mistakes and failures were pointed out as well as glories. The poetry was an integral part of this history, because singers were so highly venerated, and regarded as the truest commentators on their times. Every

47

Oudamovian had a large repertory of songs; and they customarily sang continuously to themselves when walking or working alone. All in all, a strongly traditionalist basic training, designed to inculcate attitudes not by argument or exhortation but simply by soaking the mind and heart in the most vital expressions of the community's spirit and achievement.

It will be obvious what a key part in all this was played by the training of the memory. This was not just a matter of sheer memorisation either. One of the prime objects was to make the child from earliest years an accurate witness to the events and words of every day. They used to play a game to develop this skill. One child would be sent out of the ring for a moment to think up a question, preferably as outrageous and silly as possible. Then she would come back and put the question to another boy or girl, who would have to make the most appropriate answer they could. The first child would then go round the circle collecting further answers, and all of them had to be different. The question and all the answers were written down by a grown-up. The great idea was to make them all as funny as possible, and the first time this game was played with a group the proceedings inevitably dissolved in shrieks of helpless laughter. But then, when everyone had answered, the meeting was called to order, and each child in turn was examined on what had actually been said. If the first to be interrogated got, let us say, the original question right, then the questioning would pass to the second, who would be expected to give the first answer that had been made; but if the original question was wrongly related, the questioning would go round the circle until someone remembered it correctly. Absolute exactitude was required. The child with the highest score in right answers became leader for that day, and was the one to make up the starting question the next morning. Any child who did not try seriously was in disgrace. Of course, what happened was that, as the days went by, the leader would do his very best to make the initial question funny, so that the others would laugh and not concentrate, and the rest all sat round

48

trying to attend, as solemn as judges, determined not to lose a single syllable.

This kind of training had the most irritating results. I found again and again that I was brought up short in discussion with Oudamovians of all ages, because they would counter something I had said with the words, "Just now you said so-and-so", or "The other day you said this or that". What was worse, in every case they were right or, rather, in the cases where I was doubtful I could not contradict them because my own memory was never good enough for me to be sure whether they were right or not. I am afraid I must also confess that they hardly ever had to correct each other in this way.

As usual they have a religious argument to back up their practice. God commands us, they say, to speak the truth, and to let our Yea be Yea and our Nay, Nay. Indeed, why were we given the power of speech, if not for this purpose? But how can we hope to obey these commands, unless we train our memories to the utmost? Speaking the truth is not just a matter of good intentions or courage; it also calls for accuracy in observing, listening and retaining. That is one reason why God gave us the power of memory. If we do not exercise it or if we misuse it we shall sin against love by wronging our neighbour every day of our lives.

I must say that I do now wonder, when I hear our own educationists saying that there is no need to foster memory, or even that it is positively bad to do so because it inhibits flexible and creative thought, and in any case you can always look up what you have to know, and all you really need to remember is where to find the information you want, whether this may not have incalculable effects on our moral, personal and social life? Scientific experiment has shown how hard it is to rely, for instance, on the evidence of witnesses in court. And we all know how much unhappiness can be caused in family life or between business colleagues by people who are

49

not liars or romancers—one can learn to allow for that— but just incurably inaccurate. And will not the decrying of memory make all this worse? It is not, I think, a question to be lightly brushed aside.

Six

THE benefits of life in the large multi-unit family compounds of Oudamovia did, of course, have their balancing disadvantages, the most notable of which was that at times there could be an irritating sense that nothing was private, that everyone's business was everyone else's. To an Englishman this could be very hard to take; and the Oudamovians themselves did, I suspect, have an underlying urge to compensate for this excess of sharing. Like the members of another over-public culture, the Australian aborigines, they had a safety-valve, a sort of "going walkabout". From early youth onwards all of them, girls as well as boys, would from time to time take off on their own to spend anything from twenty-four hours to a week in solitude, either in the forest or by the sea coast. They had, in fact, as I have mentioned, been trained from childhood to fend for themselves in such conditions; and it was a rigid rule to respect the privacy of someone who had thus withdrawn, at any rate until the time they announced in advance for their absence had elapsed.

It did not seem, so far as I could discover, that these times of solitude were particularly religious. Those who went on them were not, as we would say, "going into retreat" to pray or meditate. Virginia, Barnabas's daughter, trying to explain to me why she had just spent four days at the edge of the forest, overlooking the south coast, one of the wildest parts of the island, said, "I wanted to let myself come back into myself". The demands of such an outgoing life-style as the Oudamovians held up as the ideal did seem to me at times to threaten a person's sense of individual identity. This raised an interesting question about the life of heaven, and at one stage I discussed this point with them. All our images of heaven, and certainly theirs, tend to be very public ones. It is the "communion of saints", a knowing even as we are known, an eternal liturgy, a choral praise. Are we to be allowed not one secret silent thought of adoration or thanksgiving just between God and ourselves? and if not, could it really be said that I, this individual child whom God loves, still exist in any true sense to make my contribution to the total harmony of glory? The question was, I felt, a new one to them; and perhaps was thrown up in my own mind only by the centuries of modern European individualism which formed no part of their history. But thinking about it since, I am convinced it is concerned with more than our own egotistical illusions. Jesus himself was very much an individual, not a mere abstract ideal of humanity in general. Our individuality is something God intends in the magnificent multiplicity of his creation, and as such is a good thing not meant to be lost for ever. Indeed, destroy that individuality and you have no true community, for how would we ever be together again with those we have loved and lost awhile, co-operating in the dance of heaven? The words "we" and "they" would have no meaning. No, our need for solitude is not, I fancy, a mere aberration of our fallen state, but answers to something eternal.

Yet, on the other hand, our reality as persons is something that springs not from our inner resources so much as from the fact that we matter to others and are the objects of their knowing and loving. Barnabas's brother Peter remarked, when we were talking on this subject, that "those who live alone can neither give nor forgive, neither share nor receive. All these are very hard things to do well, and learning to do them can be very painful. But we must learn them if we are to become true men and women, as God wished us to become." This, I am sure, is true; but if it is true of our relations with each other, must it not be supremely true of our relation with God? In other words, does not our ultimate reality as an individual derive from the fact that *God* knows us and loves us? And will not, then, the all-pervading fact of heaven, that God knows and loves us all as his children, create simultaneously and for ever both a perfect community and for each one of us a true and indestructible individuality?

Will it not be in our reflection in his eyes that we become aware of ourselves and of those others, linked now in a delight that can never be broken? And is not this, and not the Nirvana of the Buddhist, the true reconciliation of all those beings at present alienated from one another?

But to return to Oudamovia. One thing which is quite certain is that they did not use these solitudes for what we might call "communing with Nature". Their attitude to Nature was in fact very interesting, since they did not approach her in any of the ways to which we are accustomed. They did not romanticise her, like our townsfolk brought up on nineteenth century lyric poetry, nor did they see in her merely a field for exploitation. They were not over-awed by her nor frightened nor hostile, having a sublime assurance of that immortality which her forces could never touch. But equally they showed no signs of wanting to be absorbed into her, like some mystics. Their attitude may perhaps best be labelled "sympathetic realism", but a realism which was realistic enough to see what we usually fail to see, namely that to understand Nature demands that we stretch our imaginations to breaking-point.

All too often, for example, we assume that because animals are below us in the scale of living things we can understand them, though they can never understand us. But this is mere conceit. We can observe them, and perhaps learn in time to recognise or predict some of the ways in which they usually behave, and so gain some insight into the springs of that behaviour. But as for having any idea what it is really like to be a horse or a cat or a dog or an elephant, we do not even begin to start. The fact is we cannot. There are impassable barriers between us as to experience or feeling. But it may be good for us to try to penetrate those barriers, something which our own writers do not seem to me to help us to do with any noticeable success, being apparently incapable of investing animals with anything but slightly modified human feelings. In Oudamovia I do not say that they succeeded, but they did at any rate try with some conception of the problem. Some of their most abstruse and taxing pieces—songs, stories, word-pictures, call them what you will—were on this subject, a small stock of classics added to perhaps once in a generation, but always included in those poems taught to the children from an early age, and even sung regularly as part of Oudamovian worship. Their effect on the community's whole outlook was profound. The truth they strove to bring home was that the world God has given to his creatures, the one world which they have to share, is in fact a different world to each one of them, but that the world each creature knows is equally true. We human beings, superior as we are, ought therefore to be very humble, because other creatures have truths which we can only dimly grasp, worlds we can never fully enter. And if this is so with regard to an ox or an ant, not to say a tree or a stone, how can we hope to comprehend the God who comprehends them all, to whom all worlds and truths are fully known because he made them? Some people have tried to compare our understanding of God to an animal's understanding of us. The truth is far more humiliating, namely that our understanding of God is even less adequate than our understanding of the life of our cat.

What then is our role in the world? For we do have one, just as every creature does. How did the Oudamovians expound the first chapter of Genesis, which, as I mentioned earlier, is one of the select Old Testament passages which they include in their primary teaching? Nature without Man, they say, left to itself makes its own world, lives its own life. Any changes in that world are very slow. Man enters this world, and because of God's gift of reason he can, if he so wishes, change it very quickly. Moreover, he has plans of his own which he wants to fulfil, and so is tempted to drive Nature with whip and spur to achieve his ends. But if he does, the end is havoc, disaster both for Nature, which cannot endure such change, and for himself, when Nature either rises up in wrath to take vengeance upon him or refuses him the gifts on which he is dependent. Man's weakness is that he will not stop to discover what really goes on in Nature, a study which calls for infinite patience and humility, not on the whole humanity's most notable qualities. But Nature and Man, for all their spontaneous antagonism, need each other. Man, although his intellectual and spiritual life constantly tempts him to forget it, is also an animal, rooted in Nature, starved and unhappy if he does not draw peace and strength from those roots not through reflection (that is the arrogant illusion of pure spirit coming back again) but by unreflective physical activity and contact. Nature, on the other hand, also needs Man. Left to herself she does not automatically produce what is best for life as a whole. God put Man into the world so that Man and Nature as partners, each contributing their own gift, could bring about the fulfilment of God's plan—which is why the perfect image of Paradise is not virgin soil, unexplored and uninhabited, but a garden. It is not enough, therefore, to divide the world into areas, giving Nature a free hand in some, in others Man. Man's reason was the new tool God put into the world to work toward a new and better order in which Man and Nature benefit from each other. Man "has dominion" because only he has the capacity to discover what that new order might be. But it is a humble dominion, "tilling the garden and keeping it", because Man must conform himself to what Nature can or cannot do.

Oudamovian ideas about work are in keeping with this approach. Interestingly enough, they do not have a word which corresponds exactly with our concept of "work" as such. Words for "activity" as opposed to "rest", for "craftsmanship", even for "dangerous and exhausting toil"; but not for work in general as opposed to leisure. Hence they do not think of work as a separable aspect of life, a particular necessity laid upon man which it would be nice if we could do without, but simply as an aspect of living, of the way in which man fits into the total pattern and makes his contribution, receiving in return fullness of experience growing to eternal life. Work is neither a punishment for sin, nor, in a Calvinist sense, meritorious or expiatory. It is not something inherently dull or disagreeable or degrading, which has somehow to be made interesting and invested with dignity. It is

55

an obvious part of the divine order of creation, and marked as such by God's own appointment. The plain fact is that when we look around the world there are jobs to be done, just as there were in Eden before the Fall; and those creatures qualified to do them ought to get on with them. If men behave wickedly or stupidly, then of course work becomes more and more burdensome and difficult and unproductive. But there is no virtue in doing things the hard way, or in sweating your guts out to accomplish something which is in any case misguided.

It is natural, perhaps, that they should have looked at work this way, because in the stringent conditions of life in Oudamovia, and on its relatively small scale, there was a fairly clear reason for every job, and whoever did it could see where he or she fitted in and why what they were doing really mattered. Moreover, the extreme limitation of natural resources in the island had made another enormous difference between their society and our own, namely that they had had to abandon the use of money. I say, "had to", because, as I understood it, they had done this not out of some moral revulsion against wealth as such, but simply because money inevitably created certain freedoms which they could not afford, and which could be restrained only by harsh and tyrannical laws. If a man has money, he can offer it in exchange for any commodity or service he pleases. Where the necessities of life are in critically short supply, a free market can easily exhaust them or create serious injustices in their distribution. The only way to prevent this is by detailed and repressive legislation which it is hard to enforce, and which ever increasing offers of money strongly tempt people to break. A community like Oudamovia which had to exercise the greatest ingenuity and care to survive, and whose chief asset in the struggle for survival was the free spirit of responsibility and mutual help among all its members, could afford the risk neither to its resources nor to its morale.

Instead, it was recognised that everyone had the right to food, shelter and clothing. The pattern of family life in the large homesteads made it fairly easy to ensure that there was housing for all by building to last. So long as the population remained stable the stock of homes needed renewing only very slowly. The accepted conventions about clothing, and the clever way in which the natural human desire for variety and show was satisfied, meant again that the consumption of fabrics could be predicted and controlled, and the necessary quantities supplied on request. Food was more complicated. In the farming east and the fishing west people lived on what they grew and caught. In Lohir there was an unofficial system of voluntary rationing. Each district in the city had its own market, and to this every morning came supplies of fruit, vegetables, meal, cheese, milk and fish from the outlying areas, the total quantity allotted according to the population of the particular district. In each market there was one distribution-point for each commodity. Early in the day down to the market came two or three women, with perhaps a child or so in attendance, from each household in the quarter, to make the rounds of the stalls and collect what was available. The men and women on the stalls knew everyone in the district by sight and how many folk there were in each household, and their job was to divide up the day's supply accordingly. I had been taken to visit one or two of these markets on my tour of Lohir, and very good fun they were for a student of human nature. Backchat and banter, pleading and cajolery, complaints and outright insults were all part of the game—for game it was, at bottom. Here one would be loudly alleging that her basket of fruit had more bruised ones than the load just given to her neighbour; another was claiming the imminent arrival of a son and daughter-in-law with their friend; another was trying to look all injured innocence as the stall-keepers reminded her that her parents had just gone away on a visit to the east for a month. But in the end everything sorted itself out in reasonable good humour.

One item that featured hardly at all was meat. The Oudamovians used their animals primarily for other things: wool from the sheep, milk and goat hair from the goats, leather from both when they were finally slaughtered. Protein came in the form of cheese and fish. There were no fowls, so no eggs, except for some sea-birds' eggs collected from the south-west cliffs, which could be eaten only if drenched with some strong flavour to kill the fishy taste. But the people as a whole were extremely healthy. They ate sparingly by our standards; walking and physical labour kept them strong and well-breathed; and the island was virtually germ-free. In fact, their resistance must have been nil. Had Oudamovia survived, and visitors from the outside world had found their way to it, there would have been the most appalling tragedy, because they would almost certainly have died like flies.

The population of Lohir itself consisted chiefly of craftsmen, builders and suchlike trades, and their families. The supply of materials for their work was a more centralised matter, the needs of every projected work having to be carefully calculated in advance, and, if approved, the sources earmarked. There were also a small number of scribes and other officials to keep the record of decisions taken in the national Assembly, and incorporate them where necessary in the corpus of law, and to write up the history of the people and preserve their archives. The volume of these was small—necessarily, since all had to be inscribed on skins, paper or papyrus being unavailable. The purpose of these records was in any case only to serve as master copies to decide any dispute turning on the actual substance of a law or past event. Written messages were inscribed on wax tablets, which could be smoothed and used again.

Property in Oudamovia was neither state nor privately owned in our use of those terms. The houses were given outright to the families that lived in them, who were responsible for their upkeep, and who knew indeed that replacing them would be a very serious matter. But they could not dispose of them to others; there was one use and one use only for them, to be a home for a particular family and its descendants. Public works like the roads or hot water conduits were the concern of the craftsmen appointed to build and look after them, but they were not legally vested in any corporate body. The land was divided and given into the charge of all those living in the area to use for the purpose agreed by the community. If it belonged to anyone, it was to God; but they did not make the mistake of confusing the Lord with the State. What people could have were private belongings—their clothes, their musical instruments, their tools, their fishing tackle, their works of art, and so forth, and these were the only items that could be handed down by inheritance—as indeed they were, and greatly valued too, not as antiques and museum exhibits, but for use.

All these disciplined arrangements, however, would have been of little avail, if the numbers of the Oudamovians could not have been kept stable. I was there too short a time to establish the degree of intimacy needed for them to tell me about so personal a matter, so I have no idea whether they had any particular means for avoiding conception. Their forefathers had shared the Jewish and Christian destestation of the pagan practice, normal in the Roman Empire, of exposing unwanted infants at birth; and it was obvious to anyone that the present-day Oudamovians delighted in children and welcomed their arrival. Infant mortality would, I imagine, have been higher than it is with us, for Oudamovian medicine was of the very simplest kind. They buried their dead in rock graves in the mountains, but I had no time to visit these, and so do not know whether there was a large proportion of child memorials. In any case, among such a healthy people this factor alone would not be enough to control population. It may be that their women had some intuitive awareness of fertile and infertile periods, such as some observers have claimed to detect in Samoa. But I really have no answer to this question, and can only testify that, whatever their secret, they had managed to keep their numbers at a viable level.

What is quite certain is that they had managed to combine great joy in physical love with a high standard of sexual morality. In fact, the two things went together in their outlook. Since we seem to have great problems in this matter, it may be worth giving a brief account of their own view of

59

it, as this was explained to me one evening, walking in the forest near Beresit.

That we are men and women, not just "human beings", is a fact about us which is inescapable, like the hair on our head or the colour of our eyes. A man and a woman cannot meet or speak with each other or do anything together without this truth entering in. This is a great happiness, a gift of God which fills our life with light and richness. But it does not mean that we have to make love to every man or woman we know. Indeed, if we did do so, the pleasure itself would be lost, and every friend reduced to the same level. We would not learn to know other people better, for we should see them all in the one light. The chaste man or woman can see better into the inner mysteries of the soul.

Nevertheless, the love of our bodies is a wonderful thing, one of the greatest gifts of God. We should strive always to do it well, in a way which expresses the most love and gives and receives the most pleasure. But men and women are not creatures only of flesh and blood; they are also spirits and souls. So it comes about that physical love is even more precious when it is combined with love and admiration for the other person, when it expresses these things, and goes with a desire to share every part of our life, our thoughts, feelings, ideals and deepest loyalties with them. Those who are so close in this way long to be close in other ways, and are disappointed if this cannot be so. In its turn, the love we have in the body helps us to come closer in these other ways, gives us more delight in the mind and heart of the one we love, enables us to work together with them for the good of our fellow human beings more effectually, fills our whole being with peace and trust and hope. All this happens when we love not just what is outwardly beautiful in the other person but what is inward; and when both are free to give their whole lives to each other in true partnership.

Men and women of goodwill have always known this by the light God put into their souls at the creation. But Christ taught us something more. He showed us that we are most like God when our loyalty is absolute, when love lives on even through calamity, rejection, cruelty and every sort of evil, by means of sacrifice and forgiveness. If then it is a great thing when our physical love and joy in each other's beauty gives fire and strength to a union of the soul and mind and heart, is it not an even greater thing when it does the same to a devotion like that of the Crucified himself?— when we learn, indeed, not only to forgive but to be forgiven, to receive our worth at the hands of someone who loves us, and so to be reconciled even to the evil within our own hearts? A love set firm on such a rock is one of the noblest things we can do with our lives; and if the love of the body helps to make such a life possible, then this is its greatest fulfilment. This is what Christian marriage means, and the reason why it sets us free to serve God as those who have truly known his own loving kindness towards us, shown to us through the flesh of the beloved.

But if we see that this is truly one of the best things we can do with God's gift of life, shall we not be careful to do nothing which might put it beyond our reach? If we share our bodies with many, then we have less to give to the one, and it is a longer and harder task to build up this special and profound devotion, to be the only one for them and to hold them fast as the only one for us. It can be done, but only through a painful journey of penitence and purgation. However good physical joy by itself may be (and it is good), it is not the best, it is not the raising of human life to the likeness of God himself. It is this vision of the best which must in the end keep us faithful to our wife or husband both before and after we find our way to them.

Seven

YOU will have realised by now that in Oudamovia there were very few matters which were not in some way shaped by faith in God. The simple reason for this was that they saw every facet of life as a clue which God has given us to his intentions. "Understand life", they seemed to say, "understand it at the deepest level of truth, and you will begin to understand and to share the mind of God himself".

This is something we today ought to be able to appreciate with our emphasis on the proper living of human life as the truest worship. But whereas we seem to have pushed this idea in the direction of what we call "secular Christianity", that is, by trying to replace God and the supernatural with practical morality and loving human relationships, in Oudamovia quite the opposite had happened. They had not secularised religion; they had made ordinary life sacred.

There have, of course, been human societies in plenty before now where this has happened. In the ancient world it was the rule rather than the exception. Understandably enough, we reject these cultures, because their gods were in many cases cruel, the projections of human fear and ignorance. In the same way we disown much of the Christian past, because it dried up the springs of human kindness or laid men in bondage to misery and superstition. "How great", cried the Roman poet, "are the evils to which men have been persuaded by religion!" But I could not help wondering, as I watched the Oudamovians in their daily life, whether we have not thrown away the fruit with the husk. Because unworthy gods made the sacralisation of existence a source of pain and dread, we conclude that life should not be sacralised whatever the gods are like. But surely this is illogical? Was it not precisely the saving, redeeming, transforming message of joy the Gospel brought, that when we get God right then making life sacred is not a curse but a blessing?—and that in fact we need to make it sacred in order to bring that blessing to full effect?

But perhaps the mistake did not lie there. Perhaps one essential failing of the old religions was that they did not take all life within the sphere of the sacred, but marked off two realms, the sacred and the profane, and forced men to pass to and fro between them. And perhaps the fatal error of the Church was just this, that it perpetuated this immemorial division, and so gelded the Gospel of its power. This, at any rate, I think, is how the Oudamovians saw it. To their mind, God sent his Son into the world at the time he did because men had by then developed under God's guidance a right conception and framework for understanding human life, but they did not have the right content to put into it. They knew that life should be holy, but the true nature of holiness was hidden from them. By bringing that true holiness into the world, a mighty event from which incalculable consequences have never ceased to flow, Jesus opened the way for a human society infused and governed in every part by the patient wisdom, the sacrificial love and forgiveness characteristic of God himself. This, not ritual worship or magical cleansing, was to be the sacred law and ministry of the human priesthood; and this priesthood was to be not some esoteric sacred caste, a race within a race, but the whole human family, acting as priest to the whole created order, and each man and woman acting as priest to their brother and sister.

It is after all odd, when you think about it, that in our own tradition of Christianity the doctrine of the "priesthood of all believers" should be used by some as an argument for abolishing priests, when the logical conclusion surely is that through Christ everyone is made a priest. But perhaps the reason why we have never seen this simple truth is that when the Church had the chance she did not make the sacred a matter of filling life with the heart of God, with love, loyalty, brotherhood, pardon, but simply of reinstating in a new guise the old paraphernalia of separation, cultus, and glory for the professional ministers; in short, not with priest-hood but with priestcraft. In Oudamovia things worked out very differently.

In Oudamovia there was no need for confession to a priest but only for the harder duty of confession to the person one had offended. This laid on them the priestly privilege of pardon and reconciliation, and when they had exercised this privilege, then God himself had also forgiven. Everyone had that assurance and that joy. But what if the other person would not forgive? They were quite clear about this also, extending the explicit teaching of Jesus himself. "Where one man or woman or child has forgiven another, God also has forgiven; and where a man or woman or child has confessed and not been forgiven, God has forgiven them, but the one who could not forgive has not been forgiven." That was their rule. In the same way, anyone could bless: where you bless me, God has blessed me.

This principle reached out to give sacramental value to the most ordinary acts of life. They did not, as people used to do in the ancient world, have special rites of washing to purge away sin. That, they felt, would miss the whole point. But when, after confession and pardon, they washed them-selves in the ordinary way, they saw this as an effectual sign of God's washing away the contamination of the evil they had done. A mother or father bathing their child was not just making the body clean, but putting right all that had gone wrong with the day. In just the same way, a kiss or an embrace did not establish a merely temporal bond but a unity that would endure into the next world, and help to carry us all there together.

There are many things, perhaps, which in retrospect I have read into what I saw during my all too brief sojourn in Oudamovia and which they themselves would not have said, or not said in my words. Possibly they would have brought to bear on them some trenchant criticism—almost certainly, I would say, for they were above all things balanced with that balance that comes only from the corporate wisdom of long experience, handed down from generation to generation, whereas I am still trying to put some order into my whirling thoughts. All the time I was there I was constantly being stood on my spiritual head, and I am not yet quite sure which way up things are. But I would rather have the muddled and topsyturvy ideas they started in me than all the pieties of my former life which never moved my soul.

One glimpse in particular haunts me. It seems to me now that so much of the way we commonly try to grow in holiness is nothing less than a flying in the face of grace, because it is an attempt to make ourselves into what we ought to be. This, you may say, is nothing new; we are all of us constantly warned against that. We are indeed, we are warned not to go forward in our own strength but to rely upon the power of God and of his Spirit. That is true, but it is not what I had in mind. I am thinking not only of the power but of the goal, not just of what takes us there but of where we are going.

The exercise of self-examination is one that all serious Christians try to carry out more or less regularly. We look at our lives, and we judge them by some standard—the virtues, perhaps, or the Ten Commandments, or the Sermon on the Mount, or just by some ideal of Christian behaviour we carry in our own head. We then take note of our defects and failings, and we pray to God for grace to improve. We take resolutions to be more truthful, less lazy, braver, more devout; and we try for a time to live up to a kind of projected picture of ourselves which we sketch in our minds, a basic portrait, probably none too accurate to start with, but now with the blemishes removed—a happier face, perhaps, a more disciplined programme. We are sincere in asking God to help us match this picture, but how often he does not seem disposed to do so! As the years go by, do we not find ourselves still asking for the same things . . . and not receiving them? Is grace an illusion?

No, grace is not an illusion. It is simply that we shall never find it if we look in the wrong place. The lesson we need to learn is that it is no use asking God's help to make ourselves because making ourselves is the last thing God will

65

ever help us to do. *We have to receive ourselves as a gift.* That is what the very word "grace" is all about.

We have to receive ourselves as a gift, not just at the hands of God but of man also. And it is our very self we receive, not just our thoughts, feelings, conduct. A magistrate once said to me, "When I am not sure what to make of a witness, I don't look at his face but at the faces of the other people in court". It is at other people's faces, other people's lives that we must look to guide and change our own. It is their unhappiness that must move us to penitence and amendment, not our own dissatisfaction with ourselves. I must learn to respond directly to the trouble, anxiety, disappointment they experience as a result of being bound up with me in the bundle of life. I must learn to see my opportunities in their needs, to be prompted and empowered to good by their predicament. A strong useful working body is built up by hard labour, not by inflating our muscles in front of a mirror. So it is with the soul. It grows when we are not thinking about it, and becomes something very different from and much better than we ever imagined.

It is the same with all that is good in life. It is when we lose ourselves in admiration for someone else's courage or generosity that grace flows into our soul. This is true above all of their forgiveness. True repentance is realising the simple fact that the worse our sins have been, the more amazing is the goodness that pardons them and loves them into newness of life. We ought always to be more delighted at the generosity of those who forgive us than we are distressed at the wrongdoing they have had to forgive. And this applies supremely to God's pardon. The world may think it very improper that a sinner should be happy, but if he is not, then Christ will have died in vain so far as he is concerned. Not to be happy is to care more about the fact that we are bad than the fact that God is good. And anyone whose scale of values is so inverted as that will never escape from the prison of his own ego. If our sins prove intractable, the answer (unless they are of physical or psychological origin, in which case they are not sins) will always be found to be egotism; and the cure for egotism is humility, which is not thinking badly of oneself (that may be the most ingrained form of egotism) but not thinking about oneself at all. We must be content to accept whatever value we may have as a gift from the love of others, and leave it to the last day to reveal what that value may be, for it is certain we shall never perceive it for ourselves.

In all this, grace is as usual only perfecting nature, for we all know by now, surely, that it is through relationship that we become mature human beings. And I think that these tentative and groping thoughts have sprung from my visit to Oudamovia because, as I hope I have managed to convey, theirs was a society rich in a multitude of interlocking relationships and in mutual dependence, forced on them in part by circumstances, no doubt, but all the more real for that.

Eight

DURING my stay in Oudamovia many things were said which have remained with me, obstinately refusing to fade away as good advice ought to do if it is not to become a perfect nuisance. But of all these provocative notions one has proved of especial and lasting value. It came in the course of the second and last eucharist I attended, and which I shall try to describe in a moment. A group of us were talking about one of the readings for the day, an Easter story, and in particular the words, "Behold my hands and my feet, that it is I myself", on which one of the oldest members of the community in Beresit had given the shortest Easter sermon I have ever heard.

"If we had been God, you and I", the old man said, "what would we have done when these human beings murdered our Son? Our Son who had become one of them, healed their sick, shown them the truth, rejoiced with them in their feasts, wept with them beside their graves? I will tell you. When he returned to heaven, we would have fallen on his neck and kissed him, we would have robed him in his eternal beauty, and we would have said, 'As for them, we will not care about them or think of them again. If they would not love you in your humility, they shall never rejoice in your glory.' And where should we have been then? But God is not like us. He said: 'Now I shall give you back to them, so that they may know that even their sins cannot keep us from loving them. And to show them that, you shall go back to them robed in eternity (not in your full glory for they could not bear that) but also with the marks of their nails. Then they will know that they are forgiven, and that we shall stay with them for ever.' "

That was all. Surely it was enough! But not enough for some of us. It was the Oudamovian custom to talk among

68

themselves for a while about the reading or anything that had been said about it or the feast in general, if it happened to be a feast-day. In this way they, as it were, "broke the Word" to each other. On this occasion, out of courtesy to their guest, they asked me if I had anything I particularly wanted to say to them. In fact I do not think I had, but I felt obliged to try; and so I held forth for some little time on another aspect of the text, not all that relevant to Easter, I suppose, namely how this incident showed us that sacrificial love was the very heart of the nature of God himself, true even in eternity.

When I had finished, one of the others in the group said quietly: "It is strange, isn't it, how each of us is attracted by something different in the Gospel. For me it is the teaching of Christ, so clear and firm. I like to know where I stand! For you, it is the suffering of Christ, his heroic self-denial, his Passion. I remember that you have spoken of these things before, and always your eyes are alight, your voice on fire. But I ask myself: is it the things we love in the Gospel that are good for us, or the things we hate?" He paused, then, seeing some of us look puzzled, he went on: "I love the commands. Why? Perhaps because I think that I keep them already, and so I feel proud. Or perhaps because, if I enjoy listening to them and admiring them, I feel that is enough, and I do not ask too closely whether I keep them or not. I feel that I belong at least to a disciplined army, where others keep them. In all these ways I make sure that the commands never cut me to the heart, never question me. But I do not like the parables or the puzzling things Jesus said, because they make me wonder whether I really understand him, whether I am right after all or just an ignorant child. And you: perhaps you are good at suffering, at turning the other cheek, but you might not like to think about testifying before governors and kings, or hating father and mother, wife and child. Forgive me, I do not know. But that is what I was asking myself: if we make God's Word in our own image, how will he ever make us in his?"

I do not think I have ever heard words which challenged

so toughly not only our own general attitude to spiritual things but also our customary methods of commending the faith to outsiders. But there is no need for me to spell out the point. I pass it on, simply because it is something for which I myself can never be sufficiently grateful.

We were all in the compound of one of the homesteads at Beresit, and everyone from the settlement who was not away from home was there. For the first half-hour or so people had gone around, greeting friends, enquiring after the sick, and in some cases offering apology, making reparation and seeking forgiveness for some trouble that had arisen with a neighbour. Then we had listened to songs sung by members of the village, some about creation, some about love and family, some about Easter itself; and various people, including some of the children, had stood up and told the great Easter stories. It was after this that the old man had spoken to a hushed gathering, and we had then gone on, as I have related, to speak among ourselves. Gradually this time of sharing and questioning gave place to prayer, each keeping silence or speaking as they were moved, in praise or supplication. Some were sitting or kneeling, others were standing just as their pilgrim fathers might have done in the third century, heads thrown back, hands held outwards and upwards. Then, catching it from one corner where one strong voice began, all took up the most venerable of all Christian hymns, the Trisagion. Back and forth in a kind of round it went, "Holy, holy, holy", finally dying away as Thomas, Barnabas's father, came forward to a great table in the centre of the garden. Standing there he gave thanks for all things: the world and the stars, the choirs of cherubim and seraphim, the gift of life, of good and shelter and human love. "But above all . . . "—how can I describe how he praised the love of God in his pardon and presence, in the coming down from heaven of the Son, in the Cross and in the Risen Light? At last he came to the command of Jesus in the Upper Room, ending it not where we do but with the words, "I tell you, I shall not drink again of the fruit of the vine until I drink it new with you in the king-

70

dom of God". Never have I felt so wonderfully the presence of the Risen Christ in the midst, as we all received, giving the bread and the cup to one another. Then after a time of intensest quiet we all stood up to kiss our neighbours and turn for home.

It was at this point, when quite a number of people had already left the compound, that the whole sky seemed to crack with the most tremendous grinding roar that ran from far north to far south and went on and on and on for what seemed an eternity but cannot in fact have been much more than a minute. Following immediately on this the ground beneath our feet began to tremble violently as the shock waves ran out and out from the centre of the cataclysm. Barnabas turned to me, tense and urgent: "It has come", he said, "we thought it would be some days yet. Pray God we can get you away. Quickly!"

He seized my hand, and began to lead me away from the houses down to the road, waving as he went. Out of the crowd came two men I knew well by sight but had not spoken much with, and ran to join us. "We must go at once", Barnabas shouted to them, "and see if we can reach the boat. No time to say Good-bye!"

They came without a word. God knows that I myself have wept when I remember how I was torn away from my new friends in this strange but dear land with no opportunity to say even one word of thanks or blessing, or to show how much I admired and loved them. But these were torn from wives and children, fathers and mothers, forced to leave them in the hour of last agony without so much as a clasp of farewell, simply to try to save a stranger.

Still, when sleep will not come, jagged flashes from that hellish, stumbling race strike across my sight and force my eyes open in terror. On the eastern side of the pass the road surface was not too bad, though long trails of sulphurous vapour floated down through the trees, and sometimes caught at us, half choking us. Because I could not go fast enough uphill, they took it in turns, two at a time, to support me on each side and help me along at their own loping stride. But it was when we reached the top of the pass that our real troubles began. Every few hundred yards the road was cracked across with great gaping fissures and blocked by falls of rock, over all of which they had to manhandle me. But the most sinister race of all was against the great lava stream which we could see moving down the volcano to the south of us. The whole side of the mountain facing the road was split open, and a huge molten tide welled forth as if from some unimaginable blast furnace, making straight across our path. The heat sweeping down the valley seemed to suck every last dreg of strength from one's body. But we made it.

After five hours we reached the easternmost quarter of Lohir and were able to run, or at least stagger, along firm streets. Not a soul was to be seen. "They will be at the Assembly House", shouted Barnabas, "praying". Down a gentle slope we came on to the quayside. Two men were standing there, holding the ropes of a catamaran with sail already up. I was bundled aboard, and at once all five men sprang into a canoe from which a line ran to the bows of my own craft, and began to paddle furiously, towing me out across the lagoon.

When we reached the open sea, they cast off and came alongside. Barnabas reached up and held my hand. "Come with me!" I shouted, "don't go back there!" As soon as I had said the words, I knew they were unworthy; but he never reproached me. "It will not be long", he said, "we shall meet again soon, and in a better country. Remember what we have shown you, and tell our brothers and sisters in England. And forgive us for putting you in danger." "Forgive you!" I cried, "I can never thank you enough. God the Father, God the Son, and God the Spirit, bless you and comfort you all!" Their boat dropped away. For a time they were silhouetted against the infernal glow from the island, then I saw them no more. The wind caught my sail, and I was hurled onward into the unending wilderness of the ocean.

* * *

Six weeks later I drifted ashore on the coast of southern Africa. It is late summer now, and the cove in Dorset where I am finishing my story is no longer empty as it was when it all began. But every few moments the voices of the children fade away, the sun goes in, and I am straining my eyes under a grey sky for a long brown hull that will never come again.

"O God of the ever-present crosses, help your servants. . . ."

Nine

MY entire stay in Oudamovia amounted to no more than a single fortnight, the length of an annual holiday. There is always something ridiculous about the friend who assures us that he knows all about, say, the Yugoslavs, because five years ago he went on a package holiday to Dubrovnik. I am just as conscious of the fact that there is something absurd about my confident-seeming attempt to lay bare the spiritual life of the Oudamovians after no longer an acquaintance.

Nevertheless, whether or not I have misrepresented them—and I hope and pray I have not, or not seriously at any rate, though in the light of eternity it cannot matter greatly to them now—there are questions which they have started in my mind about our own version of Christianity, and I would be betraying a trust if I did not, in conclusion, try to share some of these questions with whoever is ready to listen.

The first and obvious thing that needs to be said is that the Oudamovian vision cannot be transposed as it stands into our own situation. In the Providence of God they were taken out of the evil world. Oppression, war, poverty, degradation, all the dark side of what none the less we rightly call "civilization" passed them by. Nor did they have to wrestle with other faiths on the march, Islam, the religions of the East, sects out of Christianity by theosophy or millenarianism, atheist humanism, Marxism. It could very justifiably be objected that it was made all too easy for them to reconcile the Church and the World and to dissolve the distinction between them. It could also be said, though this ought decently to be left to those Christians who, like our brethren in communist countries, are undergoing persecution, that they have known nothing of the perennial Christian vocation (and temptation) to martyrdom. The gulf between the Church and the World is fixed not just by the indifference of those

74

who do not accept Christian faith and morals but by the active hostility of many who are implacably resolved to destroy them. In such circumstances one may be glad for the Oudamovians, but how can their experience be more to us than a Utopian dream?

These are serious questions, but they do not to my mind settle the matter. It may be that the apocalyptic vision is the true one, and that the mystery of iniquity will continue to work until God closes the book once for all. Perhaps the Kingdom of God, in this world anyway, is itself a Utopian dream. But it does not follow from this that our enemy ought to be allowed to distort the good that we maintain against him. It may be true that the forms of Christian discipleship which we have shown to the world have for the most part been forced on us by antichrist from the earliest days, that we have had no practical alternative. But that does not mean that we should hold up these imperfect forms to the world as the ideal we are asking them to embrace.

Because of our alienation from Judaism, and our indoctrination with the firm belief that the Jewish religion in our Lord's day was an inferior, particularist faith which could never measure up to God's plan of universal salvation, there is one very large and important fact which we Christians tend to forget. The situation into which God chose to send his Son was that not of a church but of a nation. Jesus spoke not to a separated people of God within a larger secular community but to a people who, though occupied by a foreign power, still recognisably were and thought of themselves as an independent secular and political entity. Scholars have debated what Jesus's attitude was to the Gentiles, and whether he paid much heed to them at all in his teaching. What we can perhaps say, from the Gospel evidence, is that he saw the Gentiles within God's loving Providence but not as a central concern of his own mission. This means then that his message was directed to the daily life of a people, not of a sect or a religious movement. His horizons may, in a human sense, have been small, but they were total. They comprehended, they did not divide. He saw response to God as the business of the whole natural community, in its day-to-day living. In this he was in the mainstream of Judaism, and it is this above all which marks him off from such enthusiasts as the sectaries of Qumran.

This vision has never been completely lost in Christianity, though it has more often than not been the hobby-horse of eccentric minorities who have tried to set up ideal Christian communities in various parts of the world. But there was a period when it became one leading idea in the thinking of a large part of christendom, and that was the Reformation. Calvin's Geneva and the Pilgrim Fathers in America are two obvious examples; and it is a pity that their repressive and limited life-style has not unnaturally become the one associated in most people's minds with this particular Christian approach to human life. For there was in fact another example, broader-based and more humane, at least in intention, and that was the Church of England. Time has made it virtually impossible for us to enter imaginatively into the ideal that irradiated the golden springtime of Anglicanism. We live in a pluralist society, where both rulers and ruled may be of any religion or none, and so "Erastian" has become a term of contempt, and Erastianism an unworkable farce. How far away it all seems to us now is witnessed, for example, by the difficulty we have in reading the Prayer for the Church Militant in the Book of Common Prayer in the spirit in which it was written. To us, much of it reads as though the Church, as the Christian organisation in England, is praying for various aspects of the secular life of the society in which it finds itself—which is indeed the attitude of the corresponding prayers in our modern liturgies. But for the men and women of the Age of Hooker it was not like that at all. The Church was simply the State at prayer; and the various petitions are asking that the people concerned shall carry out the human tasks allotted to them in God's Providence in the way he intends. The Queen comes first because the head of the natural human community is the one person in whom all aspects of its faith and life converge; and those in authority under her are severally responsible for particular and equally necessary elements in that life, whether it be the administration of justice, the conduct of government, the preaching of the Word of God, or the ministry of the sacraments. All these are facets of the life of human society as God meant it to be, and all are both natural and supernatural functions. The secular and the sacred have become one.

It is clear enough that such an ideal cannot be made to work as things are today. But to say that a thing cannot be made to work, given particular difficulties, is not to say that it is wrong in itself; and if we do say that it is wrong, we must beware lest we are merely rationalising our own fears in face of seemingly insuperable obstacles. For example, one assumption underlying the kind of ideal I have described is that Christianity is the truest and best answer to questions about the eternal order in which we live and move and have our being, and that other faiths and philosophies are wrong, or at any rate less true and less good. To take this line in a society like our own at the present time is certainly unpopular and, given the picture of a number of competing religious movements within an uncommitted secular state, arguably against the public interest. Christianity, as still the majority religion, is thus under pressure not to adopt such an attitude, and is currently agreeing to and co-operating in a variety of pluralist syllabuses for religious teaching in state schools, designed to present a number of faiths with sympathetic objectivity. This is something that many Christian teachers find it very difficult to do. Ironically enough, they might well find it easier to reconcile their own deepest commitment and their convictions about what is best for their pupils with sympathetically objective information about other religions, if they were living in an avowedly and officially Christian society, which did not, like Muslim Turkey, repress other faiths, but shaped its own life by the vision of humanity as the brothers and sisters of the Son of God.

The Oudamovian ideal is not impractical, even in our wider world. But the danger is that when we think of it in the context of that wider world the gravitational pull of our conventional ideas of Christianity subtly degrades it into just another version of the Christian mistakes of the past. We have all probably had the experience of that state between sleeping and waking when one is conscious, aware of the need to wake up and struggling to do so, but apparently paralysed. We make herculean efforts to rise from the pillow, move hand or foot, and even at times have the illusion of success, so that we may be deluded for the moment into thinking ourselves actually out of bed. Then suddenly we realise that nothing has happened and that we are still asleep. It is a strange condition to be in, and can even be frightening. I have often felt that some of the struggles of Christian theology are rather like this. We are groping for some vision, or some quite simple and obvious truth which we are sure is there, and which we feel really would change everything, would be as great and exhilarating a change as the passage from sleeping to waking. But despite all our efforts, despite all the seemingly violent and revolutionary thrashings about of our theologians, nothing ever does change. The system absorbs it all, goes serenely on, and we sink back into the same old routine with all its problems and its lack of effect. This is how I feel as I try to define and communicate what it was that Oudamovia was saying to me, why they were moved to send for me, what they wanted me to pass on.

After much striving the best I can do—and it is a poor best, I know—is this. Christians are those human beings who through Christ have had their eyes opened to the true situation of mankind as brothers and sisters of the Son of God. On that, or something very like it, I dare say we might all agree. But what does God want us to do about it? What vocation does this vision lay upon us? What Oudamovia seems to me to be saying to us is this: *our task as Christians is neither to tell our fellow men and women what they ought to do nor to set up an alternative society within mankind to show them what they ought to do, but as members of the human family to help all of us together to understand and to be what God wants us to be.*

I do not think that if I were to write till Doomsday I

could say anything more or more to the point than that. Looking at it, it seems so bald that surely it must be a mere platitude, a trite and obvious sentiment everyone takes for granted. "The mountains are in labour . . . " And yet the whole of Christian history bears witness to the fact that this has not, for most of us, been our ideal. Nor, as we look round at our Christian structures today, do they seem designed to further this ideal. Quite the contrary, most of them seem designed to divert our efforts away from it.

The story I have tried to tell does perhaps put one or two illustrations to the principle. If the conditions of their life were in many points very unlike ours, yet they had to live in little with one of our greatest problems: how to survive in a world of severely limited and rapidly shrinking resources. And vastly more complex though our way of life is, I do not think that in the end the fundamental principles of a solution will be found to be so very different from theirs: control achieved through self-discipline and involvement in the problem. But to give living force to that moral banality means re-thinking from scratch our political and social structures. The Oudamovians, it seems to me, succeeded against all the odds because their tightly controlled way of life was built on perfect communication and understanding. Everyone knew the ground-rules, everyone had a part to play which he could appreciate and with which he could identify, and everyone was encouraged and qualified to help in the shaping of decisions. This society was at once "authoritarian" and "democratic", a situation achieved by two main means: rational priorities in education, and smallness of scale. In this way values were preserved without being imposed; they remained alive. If the demands on the individual were great, yet everything was done to prevent their becoming uneven or excessive. Heroism and sacrifice were the last resort, not the first, as Christians have too often made them.

I do not think that any of the political formulas offered to us today even begin to match up to these requirements. One obvious vocation of Christians, therefore, is to engage in creative political thinking, to offer new concepts of structure

79

and citizenship which will help human beings to be human in the way God intended. Another is to ask radical and fundamental questions about that very shaky technique, economics, instead of supporting one of the competing ideologies of the moment, or trying to mend the world by exhortations to marginal charity.

But to suggest that the lesson of Oudamovia could be fulfilled by formulating programmes, however brilliant, would be to betray her. Grace comes to us not through abstract theories but through actual people and situations. We must learn to *think human,* to be concerned not with survival as a Church, but with co-operation in service as part of the human family. And our unique and vital contribution to that is Christ's own gift of bringing all life within the sphere of the sacred. The joy and thanksgiving that come with penitence and pardon, prayer and sacrament must not be confined to the cultic enclosure or the priestly caste but come into the lives of all men, wherever the life of God's world finds them. When the Christian family welcome into their home some-one of another faith and philosophy with whom they have been working and thinking and suffering for the benefit of the whole human family in their town or village or country, and share with them as honoured guests the bread that has been broken and the cup which has been blessed as the heart of the family meal, then Jesus Christ the eternal Son and Brother will be present in the midst—not just of his Church but of his world.